Popular Tropical Fish for your aquarium

Edited by Cliff Harrison

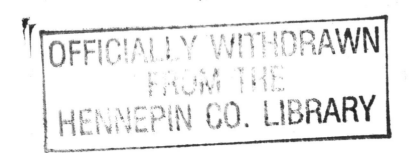

OFFICIALLY WITHDRAWN
FROM THE
HENNEPIN CO. LIBRARY

TAB **TAB BOOKS Inc.**
BLUE RIDGE SUMMIT, PA 17214

HENNEPIN COUNTY
LIBRARY

JUN 24 1985 9

FIRST EDITION

FIRST PRINTING

First published in the U.S.A. in 1984 by TAB BOOKS Inc.

Printed in Hong Kong

Reproduction or publication of the content in any manner, without express permission of the publisher, is prohibited. No liability is assumed with respect to the use of the information herein.

Copyright © 1982 by W. Foulsham & Company Limited

Library of Congress Cataloging in Publication Data

Main entry under title:

Popular tropical fish for your aquarium.

    Includes index.
    1. Tropical fish—Identification. 2. Tropical fish.
3. Aquariums. I. Harrison, Cliff.
SF457.P64 1984   639.3'4   83-4955
ISBN 0-8306-1631-4 (pbk.)

Cover photograph by kind permission of Tetra (Warner-Lambert Pet Care)

Contents

Introduction

It is intended that this book should be used mainly by the aquarist as an identification guide to enable him to decide which of the many species of freshwater tropical fish available would be best suited to him. However, this brief introduction to keeping freshwater tropical fish will serve to whet the appetite of the aspiring tropical fish keeper and provides all the essential knowledge that is required. The task of creating and maintaining a simulated natural environment within the confines of a small aquarium should not be a problem for the aquarist who is prepared to set up his tank carefully and to make regular tests to ensure that a balance is being maintained. Once a suitable environment has been achieved, the successful breeding of fish and the fascination of watching the fry develop is ample reward for the time and trouble taken.

A well-balanced aquarium has fish swimming at all levels, with plants and rockwork to provide cover.

The aquarium

Nowadays most aquaria are made from sheets of glass glued together with a special material called silicone rubber. As a result they do not leak even after many years in service, or by being emptied and refilled many times over.

The cheapest types have the visible edges of the glass smoothed and polished, whilst the more expensive ones have decorative frames of anodized aluminium or plastic with lighting hoods to match. It is possible to buy moulded plastic tanks, often in bow-fronted or other unusual shapes. These cannot be recommended for several reasons, the main ones being that they scratch easily (thereby spoiling the view of what is contained within), and they are generally available only in rather small sizes that are not really suitable for a permanent display of tropical fish.

The most popular sizes are 24in long by 12in wide by 15in high (60cm long × 30cm wide × 38cm high); and 36in long by 36in wide by 36in high (90cm long × 90cm wide × 90cm high). Within reason, obtain the largest aquarium you can afford; surprising as it may seem, it really is much easier to keep fish healthy and happy in a 36in (90cm) long aquarium that in one half the size. (N.B. tanks are usually referred to by their imperial sizes. Metric sizes are approximate.)

To support the aquarium you will need a sturdy base of some description. Special stands made of angle-iron are available to suit most sizes of aquarium, or perhaps you might prefer to make one yourself with bricks cemented together, or lightweight building blocks with a blockboard top.

Wall-mounted shelves, or lightweight modern cabinets, are just not suitable for supporting an aquarium. Remember that even a modest size of aquarium, filled with water, will weigh as much as an adult, so don't take chances.

Do ensure that the aquarium will sit absolutely flat and level on the stand, using small packing pieces of hardboard if necessary, otherwise the water level will appear to slope from one end of the tank to the other.

Because the glass can crack if the aquarium is not supported evenly at all points, it is essential to place 2.5cm (1in) wide strips of expanded polystyrene (cut from plain ceiling tiles) all around the edge of the aquarium where it is in contact with the stand. Never try to carry the aquarium when there is any water, gravel or rocks remaining in it; not only is it very heavy but a wet aquarium is very slippery and can so easily be dropped.

Siting and setting up the aquarium

When siting the tank, consideration should be given to the proximity of electrical sockets as they will be needed to supply power to the various electrical equipment required. A full tank of water is extremely heavy and cannot be moved without risking distortion of the frame and consequent damage to the glass. The tank should be sited away from direct sunlight unless adequate shading can be provided, since too much sun causes the uninhibited growth of algae and, in small tanks, may cause overheating of the water. If you are a heavy smoker it is best to site your tank in a room which is not constantly in use, as your fish will not take kindly to stale smoke-laden air which can also cause a scum on the water surface. Newly glazed tanks should be filled slowly, after cleaning the glass (do not use proprietary cleaners).

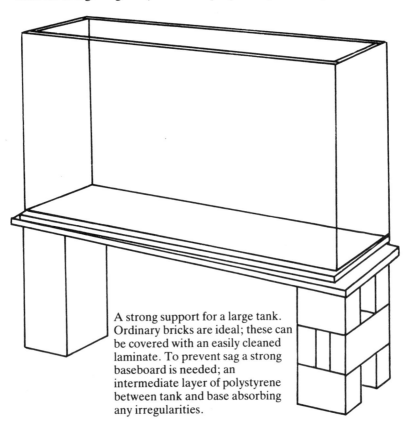

A strong support for a large tank. Ordinary bricks are ideal; these can be covered with an easily cleaned laminate. To prevent sag a strong baseboard is needed; an intermediate layer of polystyrene between tank and base absorbing any irregularities.

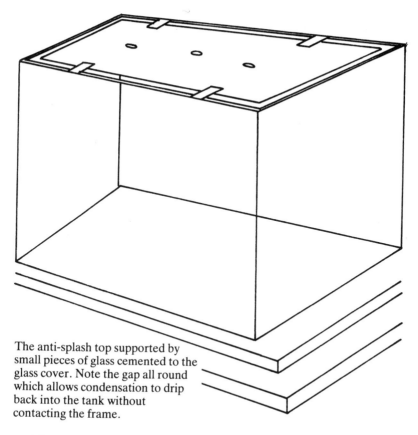

The anti-splash top supported by small pieces of glass cemented to the glass cover. Note the gap all round which allows condensation to drip back into the tank without contacting the frame.

After the tank has been set up on its stand, some consideration must be given to the cover. The aquarium cover is necessary to keep dust and dirt out and also to provide a shade for the lighting. Between the cover and the tank it is usual to put an intermediate cover of plastic or glass. This is to prevent condensation from forming on the underside of the cover and on the electrical fittings. The see-through cover should be cut 1cm (½in) smaller all round the tank top and supported on small lugs that can be glued into position. This gap allows condensation to drip back into the tank without contact with the frame. The outer cover containing the electric lighting equipment can easily be made from sheet aluminium. Alternatively, covers to fit standard size tanks are readily available from suppliers of aquatic equipment. It is advisable to have a small hole through the lighting cover, with a hole immediately below this in the condensation cover. This will enable you to feed the fish without removing the tank cover. Very large tanks can have specially constructed wooden covers. These should be made in several pieces which can be moved separately. When the tank has been sited, check that it is level with a spirit level. Any variation should be corrected by packing the supporting legs – not the tank itself.

Furnishing the aquarium

Exactly how you furnish your tank is dependent on the natural habitat of the fish that you intend to keep. The composition of the material that covers the bottom of the tank is very important. Fish generally prefer a dark bottom covering and seem to thrive better in tanks that provide this. Conversely, in tanks that provide a light coloured base the fish are restless and their coloration suffers. Since most aquarium plants are able to absorb nutrients from their leaves the floor covering medium is not so important to them as long as it provides firm anchorage for the roots. Exceptions are *Cryptocoryne* and most of the *Aponogeton* and *Echinodorus* species as these take their nourishment through their roots.

The undergravel filter, if used, should first be placed in position. The filter should be of sufficient size to cover at least two thirds of the base area. The filter is covered with gravel of ⅛in or ³⁄₁₆in grade to an optimum depth of 5–7cm (2–3in). If smaller gravel or sand is used there is a danger that the filter will become blocked, rendering it ineffective. The subject of filters is described in detail on pages 18 and 19.

A variety of materials can be used to decorate the aquarium, but you should try to create as natural an environment as possible. Some rocks, for instance, granite, slate, Westmoreland and sandstone are especially suited to aquarium use. Others, including ore-bearing rocks and limestones, are unsuitable as they are semi-soluble. Outcrops of suitably placed rocks can be used to conceal aquarium heaters and filter pipes. Rocks can also be scattered around the aquarium floor. In tropical rivers there is usually an abundance of tree trunks, twigs and branches that have fallen into the water and decayed. Therefore, pieces of wood in the aquarium, suitably weighted down, help to recreate this natural environment. Because there is no flow of water in the tank, and because the volume of water is much smaller, the wood needs to be free from decay, or pollution of the water can occur. Suitable woods are roots of beech, pine, oak and willow; preferably those that have already been in water for a considerable time. It is a good idea to boil the pieces of wood before introducing them into the aquarium, since this will kill any harmful bacteria or insects that may be concealed.

The floor covering of the aquarium is usually sloped down from the back towards the front as, besides providing a more interesting view, it allows debris to collect at the lowest point from where it can be removed easily. There is, however, no real reason why slopes cannot be made towards one corner or from the centre to each side. When filling the tank, place a small bowl in the bottom and pour the water carefully into this, allowing the water to trickle gently over the sides. This will avoid disturbance of your bottom-covering material. When the bowl is submerged completely, then pouring can continue more quickly.

When choosing your plants consideration should be given to the fish that you will be keeping and the water conditions that you will be providing for them. Reference should be made to the section on plants before purchasing, as some species will not grow well with others. The breeding habits of your fish will also affect the choice of suitable plants!

In nature, fish do not swim together except through choice. They are able to avoid community life if they prefer a solitary existence. Also, their natural habitat may have had many facets that were constantly changing – sometimes dark and forbidding, sometimes bright. Again, the fish can choose between light and shade, and where possible these choices should be given to the inmates of your tank. Any book about fish is based partly on personal observations and partly on the recorded experience of others. In consequence occasional errors of fact can be passed on. You should try to learn about your own fish and record their likes and dislikes. In a large tank it should be possible to give them a choice of environment; a shady, dimly lit corner with plenty of rocky caves, tangled branches or growths of plants where they can retire, safe from the unwanted attentions of other fish. The light can gradually increase to full brilliance at the other end and nearer the surface and it will soon become apparent which degree of illumination is preferred by the different fish in your tank.

The aquarium bottom should be sloping or undulating.

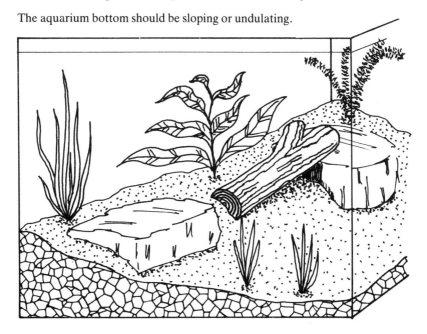

The water

Tropical fish are remarkably tolerant of a wide range of water conditions, and will almost certainly be perfectly happy in ordinary tapwater provided you leave it to 'age' for a day or two before introducing them into the tank. This ageing can be important, for it will allow harmful chlorine to escape from the water, and will also ensure that the heating and filtration systems are working properly.

There will be times when tapwater will not be suitable for a particular situation. There are a small number of species, such as members of the Killifish family, that much prefer soft, slightly acid water. You might want to breed some of the more difficult egglayers, and soft water will often be all the encouragement they need. In these cases you can use rainwater gathered from a clean, unpolluted water butt, and mix it with tapwater until you achieve the required water quality. Do remember that ordinary gravel and many types of rock will slowly dissolve in the water, making it harder. Use a special type of inert gravel if you wish to keep the water soft.

You can slightly acidify the water by soaking peat in it for a few days, or by making up a small nylon bag containing peat and placing it in the filter.

Fish do not like sudden changes in hardness or acidity, so use a water testing kit to monitor the exact chemical composition of the water. The best advice must always be to leave the water in a display tank alone: any changes you make are likely to be only temporary, and as such can do much more harm than good.

Green water Occasionally, the water might become green. This greenness is caused by the multiplication of algae and although it is a nuisance as it limits visibility, it does not constitute a danger to the fish or plants. The remedy is simple. Switch off your lights for a few days and thereafter reduce lighting until a clean water balance is maintained. Provided your plants are healthy, it is a problem you are rarely likely to experience. Algae growth on the glass can be removed by scraping with a razor blade. Careful positioning of the lighting should avoid this problem.

Evaporation All tanks lose water steadily through evaporation, and this loss should be replaced regularly before it becomes too severe.

Debris that falls to the bottom of the tank does no harm and gives the tank an established appearance. It should not be allowed to become too thick, however, and if necessary it can easily be syphoned off, creating as little disturbance as possible.

conversion tables

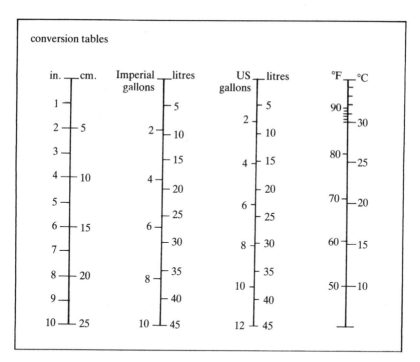

in.	cm.	Imperial gallons	litres	US gallons	litres	°F	°C
1			5		5	90	
2	5	2	10	2	10		30
3			15		15	80	
4	10	4	20	4	20		25
5			25	6	25	70	20
6	15	6	30	8	30	60	15
7			35	10	35		
8	20	8	40		40	50	10
9							
10	25	10	45	12	45		

Above: Use these tables for any conversions of sizes, quantities or temperatures you may wish to make. Below: When filling a tank, pour water onto a saucer or dish to avoid disturbing gravel.

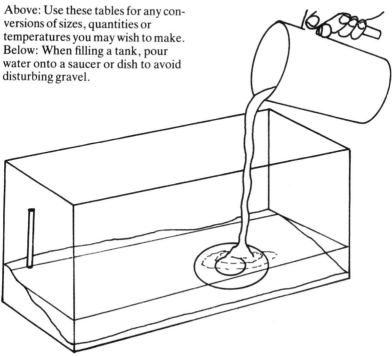

Plants in the aquarium

A well planted aquarium is not only attractive to look at, but easier to maintain. Plants take carbon dioxide from the water and convert it by a process of photosynthesis into oxygen, most of which is released into the water. This photosynthesis takes place only when the aquarium is illuminated. The amount of light required by plants varies from one species to another. Most aquatic plants are able to extract nutrients from the water through their leaves and do not rely on their roots for this function. There is also a wide range of plants that are able to extract nutrients with both roots and leaves and these are usually the easiest to grow in an aquarium. In order to thrive, some plants need calcium and others do not. Plants are therefore divided into two groups; calciphilous plants, which are those needing calcium and, consequently, hard water, and those that are calcifugous and require soft, slightly acid water. Obviously, plants from both groups will not do equally well in the same tank. Generally speaking, calcifugous plants should be chosen.

Before planting, any damaged or browning leaves should be cut off and the root tips trimmed to stimulate production of fresh root shoots. Correct planting is important and use should be made of a planting stick. Plants are very buoyant and may need stones or lead weights placed around the stem to hold them down until the roots are firmly anchored. Plants should be grouped towards the rear and sides of the tank, keeping the front free for swimming. It is better to buy two or three plants from each species, rather than single plants from a lot of different species. They are best planted in groups – all one species together, as this makes for a more natural looking arrangement. Give your plants room to grow according to their growth rate. Correctly planted and established plants should grow well and produce new leaves regularly. If your plants are small and lack growth, it is likely that the water is too hard and requires the addition of distilled water, or rainwater, to soften it. Algae growth on the leaves inhibits growth, but is difficult to remove successfully. Excessive algae growth can be caused by too much light and also by too much calcium in the water – both possibilities should be checked. The excessive use of peat extract can also inhibit plant growth, and its use must be strictly controlled.

Calciphilous plants:	Calcifugous plants:
Vallisneria (fast growing)	**Cabomba**
Elodea	**Cryptocoryne**
Sagittaria (fast growing)	**Echinodorus**
Myriophyllum	**Marsilea**

Some plants suited for aquaria

Acorus gramineus var *pusillus*
(Japanese Dwarf Rush).
Thin sword-shaped leaves radiate
from this attractive plant. A
variegated variety with
yellow-striped green leaves is also
most attractive. They prefer a well lit
tank and water at around
15–25 deg C (59–77 deg F).

Aponogeton elongatus
Easy to grow, flowers freely.
Grows to 28cm (11in).
Prefers well lit position.

Aponogeton fenestralis
(Madagascar Lace Plant).
Easy to grow.
Grows to 38.5cm (15in).
Does well in new aquaria and prefers
a soft, slightly acid water.
Prefers shady position.
Temperature range 18–22 deg C
(65–72 deg F).

Aponogeton undulatus
Grows to 23cm (9in).
Slow grower, ideal for small aquaria.

Cabomba aquatica
A beautiful plant but often difficult
to maintain successfully.
Prefers brightly lit position.

Ceratopteris thalictroides
(Indian Fern).
Grows to 0.6m (2ft).
Thrives in soft, slightly acid water.
Prefers bright light, and water of
21 deg C (70 deg F).

Cryptocoryne affinis
(Water Trumpet).
Leaves about 15cm (6in) long.
A very attractive aquarium plant.
Propagation is by runners.
Optimum temperature 25 deg C
(77 deg F).
Requires subdued light and soft
water, rather a slow grower.

Cryptocoryne beckettii
Attractive, undulating leaves grow
to about 28cm (11in).
Temperature 21 deg C (70 deg F)
plus. Prefers subdued light, slow
grower.

Echinodorus berteroi
(Cellophane Plant).
Grows to 76.5cm (30in).
Prefers soft water with tannin.
Temperature 20 deg C (68 deg F).
Well lit position.

Echinodorus paniculatus
(Giant Amazon Sword).
Grows to 51cm (20in) in good light
and, therefore is more suited to a
large aquarium.
Propagation is by runners.
Prefers soft water.
Temperature 20 deg C (68 deg F).
Easy to propagate.

Echinodorus tenellus
Grows to 7.5cm (3in).
A useful plant for small aquaria.
Develops numerous runners.
Easy to propagate.
Soft water, peat filtration.
Prefers well lit position.
Will withstand lower temperatures
around 15 deg C (59 deg F).

Egeria densa
Easy to grow. Prefers brightly lit position with some sun.
Temperature anywhere between 10–18 deg C (50–65 deg F).
Good oxygenator.

Elatine macropoda
Delicate plants which, due to their very small size, are ideally suited to smaller aquaria, although they are difficult to grow.
Prefer a brightly lit position.

Eleocharis acicularis
(Hairgrass).
Grows to an average of 13cm (5in).
This plant forms thick mats ideal for breeding tanks where egg scatterers are bred. Brightly lit position.
Propagation is by runners.

Elodea canadensis
(Canadian Waterweed).
Easy to grow but is more suited to cold water tanks as it becomes more spindly in tropical aquaria.
However, it is widely available and often seen in aquaria as it is a good oxygenator.
Will tolerate a wide temperature range 14.5–20 deg C (58–68 deg F) but will die in higher temperatures.

Fontinalis gracilis
(Willowmoss).
Very small bright green leaves attach to long filamentous stems.
Does well in good light, providing cover for plant spawners.
Low to moderate temperature preferred.
Temperature 10–18 deg C (50–65 deg F).

Ludwigia alternifolia
Grows to 15cm (6in).
An excellent aquarium plant. Easy to grow.
Brightly lit position.
Temperature 18–25 deg C (64–77 deg F).

Ludwigia natans
Prefers soft water.
Well lit position. Temperature 18–25 deg C (64–77 deg F).

Myriophyllum brasiliense
(Water Milfoil).
Grows to 1.2m (4ft).
A free growing plant that requires brightly lit position.
Propagation by cuttings.
Temperature 20–25 deg C (68–77 deg F)

Nomaphila stricta
(Giant Hygrophila).
Propagates by cuttings. Prefers well lit position in deep aquarium.
Temperature 20–30 deg C (68–86 deg F).

Riccia fluitans
(Riccia).
Grows well in water 14–25 deg C (57–77 deg F).
Forms a thick mat which floats at the surface providing good cover for fry and for spawning.

Sagittaria eatonii
Grows to 15cm (6in).
Runners for dense mats. A slow grower.
Well lit, sunny position.
Do not plant with *Vallisneria*.

Sagittaria latifolia
A robust, easily grown plant.
Only suited to very large aquaria.
Temperature range 15–25 deg C (59–77 deg F).

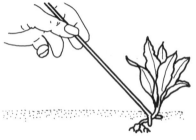

Using a planting stick.

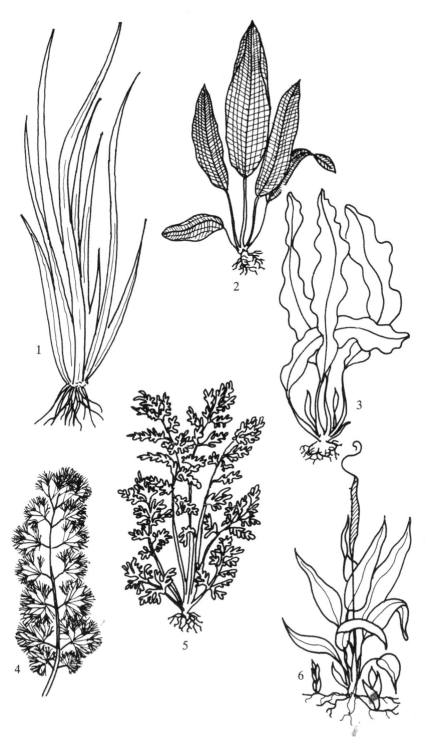

1

2

3

4

5

6

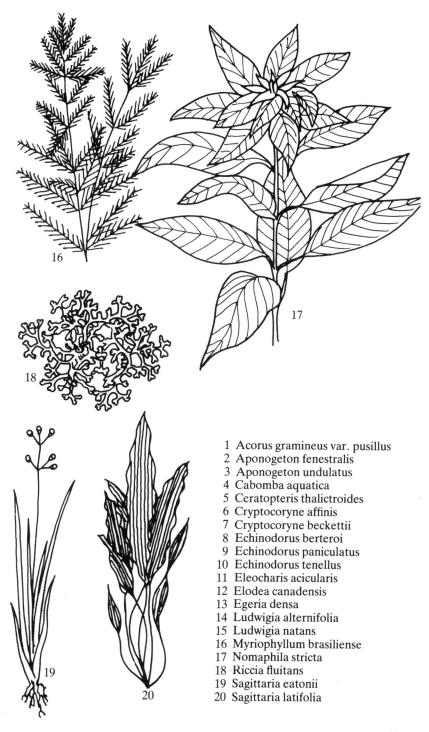

1 Acorus gramineus var. pusillus
2 Aponogeton fenestralis
3 Aponogeton undulatus
4 Cabomba aquatica
5 Ceratopteris thalictroides
6 Cryptocoryne affinis
7 Cryptocoryne beckettii
8 Echinodorus berteroi
9 Echinodorus paniculatus
10 Echinodorus tenellus
11 Eleocharis acicularis
12 Elodea canadensis
13 Egeria densa
14 Ludwigia alternifolia
15 Ludwigia natans
16 Myriophyllum brasiliense
17 Nomaphila stricta
18 Riccia fluitans
19 Sagittaria eatonii
20 Sagittaria latifolia

17

Filtration and aeration

Filtration To ensure the removal of debris from the water and to assist the breakdown of harmful waste, an effective filtering system is required. There are basically two types of filter systems that have been proved effective and trouble-free for the tropical fish keeper. These are the undergravel 'biological' filter and the mechanical filter.

The undergravel filter has proved to be simple and reliable in small and medium sized tanks, particularly where the number of fish kept is small. It comprises a perforated plastic plate that sits on small projections which hold it about 1.5cm (⅝in) off the aquarium bottom. An air lift connected to this plate causes water to be drawn from beneath it and fresh water to be drawn through the plate and the covering gravel to replace it. This flow of water draws with it any suspended matter in the water, depositing it in the gravel where it is quickly broken down by bacterial action into harmless chemicals. The grain size and depth of material covering the filter is important. It should be about the size of rice grains and have a depth of at least 5cm (2in) with an optimum depth of 7.5cm (3in). One of the disadvantages of the undergravel filter is that it will need cleaning when it becomes choked. This may only need to be done after a year, or even two years, in a tank with few fish in it, but it will mean that the tank must be completely disarranged in order to clean the filter satisfactorily. The filter should cover two thirds of the tank base if it is to operate with maximum efficiency.

Mechanical filtration involves passing the water through a layer of nylon floss that traps all the solid waste matter. Once a week, or more often if necessary, you must remove the filter from the aquarium and wash out or replace the nylon floss.

There are many different designs of mechanical filter, some being small rectangular boxes that sit inside the aquarium (bottom filters), others clipping to the outside of the aquarium where they do not interfere with the display that you have created. Usually they are air operated, but the most powerful (and expensive) ones incorporate motorized water pumps; these are generally known as power filters, and are especially useful on aquaria 36in (90cm) long or larger.

Aeration Although a certain amount of aeration is provided by the operation of the filter, there is much to recommend the use of an air pump to provide streams of fine bubbles to help stir the water even further. It is certain that vigorous aeration is helpful to the well-being of fish and aids the dispersal of carbon dioxide which might prevent the saturation of the water with oxygen.

Air pump A strong, powerful air pump is needed to operate both the airstone (see below) and the aeration filter. If both units are to be operated from one pump, a valve with outlets to divide the output between them will be required. It may be better to use two separate pumps, then if one should fail the other can take over until a replacement is obtained.

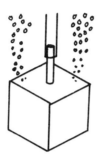

An airstone (left) and an under-gravel filter (below).

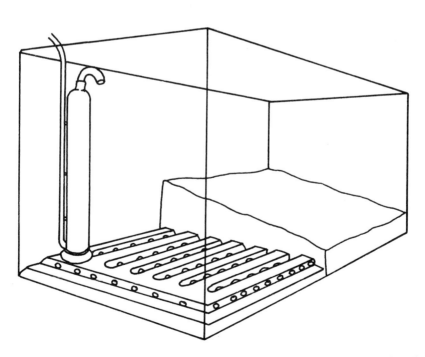

Heating and lighting

It is extremely important to maintain a constant temperature in your tank. In tropical areas the water temperature varies only by narrow margins from day to day, possibly only 1 or 2 degrees. An aquarium heater will be needed to maintain a temperature of 24.5–26 deg C (76–78 deg F). This temperature range is ideal for most aquarium fish species, although the requirements of some species are different. A large tank will probably require two or three separate heaters to provide even heating throughout, connected to a single, external thermostat. Two or three heaters are no more extravagant than using one as with thermostatic controls they are in operation for far shorter periods of time and are therefore less liable to failure. Heaters are available in different wattages to suit tanks of differing sizes. Although heaters are available with thermostats incorporated in them, it is a wise precaution to have a separate thermometer from which the tank temperature can easily be seen. It should not be positioned directly above a heater. Heaters with reliable controls are essential if the temperature is to be maintained within close limits. Always take safety precautions before touching your electrical equipment. Turn off the power before making adjustments. If in doubt, consult a qualified electrician.

Lighting in your tank is essential if you are to show your fish to their best advantage. The hood covering the aquarium hides the lighting fixtures from view and serves to direct the light downwards. A wooden top can easily be made by the home handyman and the inside surface can be covered with baking foil to reflect the light. Remember that this foil may also conduct electricity so it is important than your lampholders are adequately insulated. It is better to use warm white or white tubes which provide a much more pleasant light than daylight tubes. If the tank is placed in a position where it will benefit from 2 or 3 hours of diffused sunlight daily, this is a great help in promoting plant growth. Ordinary light bulbs can be used instead of tubes. Two 40 watt bulbs is normal for a tank of 24in (60cm) × 15in (38cm) × 12in (30cm).

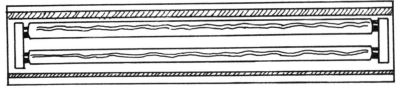

Underside view of tank cover showing fluorescent lighting – an increasingly popular method of providing even illumination.

Buying your fish

When purchasing a fish you should look for a specimen that shows erect fins, bright colours and which has a well fed look. Avoid fish that have sunken bellies or those that constantly rub themselves against rocks, as this could be a sign of irritation caused by some disease. If any of the occupants of a tank look sick then it is likely that all the fish are carriers even though the disease may not be evident in all the fish in the tank. When purchasing for the first time, do not be persuaded to buy species about which you know nothing. It is better to go out with the intention of buying specific species that are known to be compatible.

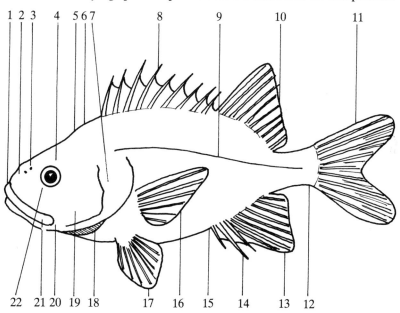

1 Premaxillary
2 Snout
3 Nostrils
4 Interorbital space
5 Occiput
6 Nape
7 Opercular lid
8 Spiny dorsal fin
9 Lateral line
10 Soft dorsal fin
11 Caudal fin

12 Caudal peduncle
13 Anal fin
14 Spiny anal fin
15 Anus
16 Pectoral fin
17 Pelvic fin
18 Gill membranes
19 Preopercle
20 Isthmus
21 Maxillary
22 Suborbital region

Parts of a fish

Try to buy locally – the journey home will be shorter and the shock to the fish much reduced. Take a polystyrene lined box with you to retain the heat in the polythene water bag. Avoid unnecessary jarring and vibration and handle your fish carefully. Choose specimens that are bright and active. Before leaving the shop, get as much information as you can. Find out how long the fish have been at the shop, where they came from and what they are eating. Also enquire as to the pH of the water in which they have been kept. Observe whether they are aggressive towards other fish and whether they have territorial inclinations.

It is far better to make a preliminary sortie to the shop on a fact-finding mission. Discuss with the shop-keeper the fish that you intend to purchase. Most are delighted to discuss all aspects of fishkeeping with a prospective customer. After all, you may become a regular purchaser at the shop which gives you an informed and personal service. Beware, however, of the dealer who is not prepared to discuss his fish with you. There are some dealers whose knowledge is not what it should be and whose only purpose is to make a sale before their badly kept fish die in their tanks. Fortunately, these dealers are in the minority and their policy is a short sighted one as the buyer will not return to their shop again. If you follow the principles of good purchasing and set out to buy only the species for which you have planned a home then you should not encounter any problem that cannot be solved by careful maintenance.

When you return home with your purchases, they should be introduced to their new environment gradually. The room lights should be dimmed, the tank lights switched off. The polythene bag containing the fish should be floated in the water for about 20 minutes to allow the temperatures to equalise. Remember to open the top of the bag or the fish may suffer from lack of oxygen. Allow the water in the bag to mix gradually with the tank water and avoid any sudden change which might occur if the pH factors vary. Newly introduced fish usually seek the shelter of plants and they should be left alone for some hours, after which they may be coaxed from their cover by offering tempting morsels of food. Any food lying uneaten should be siphoned from the tank to avoid pollution. Remember to drop the food over a clear spot in the tank so that it can easily be recovered if necessary. Keep watch on newly purchased fish and see if they are aggressive or worried by other fish. If they are not compatible one or another of the fish should be moved to another tank. A well balanced community of fish can be obtained by choosing a mixture of bottom-living species, shoaling midwater species and surface-living species. In this way, they each have their own territory and the tank has a well filled look. Where possible, you should buy fish in pairs, or even more with the shoaling fish.

Although most species of fish can be safely kept together, those denoted thus (†) in the descriptive section are species which are not recommended for the normal community tank.

When you make your choice of fish for the aquarium, there are two important considerations that must be borne in mind. First is the maximum number of fish that your aquarium will safely contain, for if you overstock then there will be insufficient oxygen, and they will soon be gasping at the surface. For tropical aquaria, you should allow approximately 25in (63cm) of fish (combined lengths) to each square foot (929 sq cm) of water surface. You must assess the fish lengths on the sizes given in this book for adult specimens, remembering that the young fish you buy will soon grow if you care for them properly.

The second consideration is the characteristics of the fish you select; it is not just whether they will all live peacefully together that is important, but also the overall effect that will be created in the aquarium. If you are setting up a community aquarium you will want fish at all levels: some staying mainly near the surface, others in mid-water, and a few remaining near the bottom. You will probably also want fish with a wide variety of behaviour patterns: for instance, some being fast-swimming shoaling types, others being more solitary in their activities. The following selections should be taken as a guide to help the hobbyist achieve an attractive and lasting display. They include fish which are all compatible, but have varied habits and appearance. The actual choice of fish is always a matter of personal taste, coupled with availability of particular species, so where preferred any of the fish mentioned can be substituted with a similar number of others that are comparable in terms of size and behaviour.

Tank selections

Tank size:
18in × 12in × 12in high
(45cm × 30cm × 30cm) – very
small, peaceful fish for the small tank

2 *Corydoras hastatus*
2 *Colisa chunae*
4 *Barbus gelius*
4 *Rasbora maculata*
2 *Nannostomus marginatus*
4 *Heterandria formosa*
8 *Cheirodon axelrodi* or
Paracheirodon innesi
4 *Rasbora heteromorpha*
2 *Acanthopthalmus semicinctus*

Tank size:
24in × 12in × 15in high
(60cm × 30cm × 38cm) – small,
very peaceful fish

6 *Cheirodon axelrodi* or
Paracheirodon innesi

6 *Rasbora heteromorpha*
4 *Hemigrammus erythrozonus*
2 *Corydoras julii*
2 *Barbus titteya*
2 *Barbus oligolepis*
2 *Colisa lalia*
4 *Brachydanio rerio*
4 *Hasemania marginata*

Tank size:
24in × 12in × 15in high
(60cm × 30cm × 38cm) – medium-
sized peaceful fish

2 *Barbus nigrofasciatus*
1 *Epalzeorhynchus kallopterus*
4 *Acanthopthalmus semicinctus*
4 *Aphyocharax rubripinnis*
2 *Colisa labiosa*
2 *Corydoras aeneus*
2 *Gymnocorymbus ternetzi*
2 *Nematobrycon palmeri*
2 *Rasbora pauciperforata*

Tank size:
24in × 12in × 15in high (60cm ×
30cm × 38cm) – medium-sized fish,
more boisterous, but not aggressive

6 *Barbus tetrazona*
2 *Corydoras nattereri*
1 *Labeo bicolor*
4 *Brachydanio albolineatus*
4 *Hemigrammus caudovittatus*
4 *Rasbora trilineata* or *Thayeria
obliqua*

Tank size:
24in × 12in × 15in high (60cm ×
30cm × 38cm) – mixed-size fish
(some large, some small), peaceful
natures

2 *Trichogaster leeri*
2 *Corydoras julii*
2 *Barbus conchonius*
2 *Barbus semifasciolatus*
6 *Brachydanio nigrofasciatus*
6 *Cheirodon axelrodi*
4 *Hemigrammus rhodostomus*
4 *Hyphessobrycon rosaceus*

Tank size:
24in × 12in × 15in high
(60cm × 30cm × 38cm) – small
to medium-sized fish, with
the emphasis on livebearers

2 *Poecilia velifera*
4 *Poecilia sphenops*
6 *Xiphophorus maculatus*
4 *Hyphessobrycon pulchripinnis*
2 *Barbus nigrofasciatus*
2 *Corydoras paleatus*
2 *Hemigrammus ocellifer*
2 *Barbus stoliczkanus*
4 *Brachydanio frankei*

Tank size:
36in × 12in × 15in high (90cm ×
30cm × 38cm) – medium to large
community fish for the larger tank

2 *Barbus everetti*
2 *Callichthys callichthys*
2 *Cichlasoma festivum*
4 *Danio malabaricus*
2 *Labeo bicolor*
2 *Trichogaster trichopterus*
4 *Xiphophorus helleri*

Tank size:
36in × 12in × 15in high
(90cm × 30cm × 38cm) – mixed-size
peaceful fish for the larger tank

10 *Cheirodon axelrodi* or
Paracheirodon innesi
2 *Corydoras julii*
4 *Acanthophthalmus semicinctus*
4 *Barbus oligolepis*
4 *Barbus titteya*
6 *Brachydanio rerio*
2 *Trichogaster leeri*
6 *Hyphessobrycon rosaceus*
4 *Nannostomus trifasciatus*
4 *Rasbora heteromorpha*

Tank size:
24in × 12in × 15in high (60cm ×
30cm × 38cm) – angel fish display

6 *Pterophyllum scalare*
2 *Corydoras nattereri*
4 *Barbus ticto*
1 *Botia macracanthus*
4 *Hyphessobrycon pulchripinnis*
2 *Kryptopterus bicirrhis*
4 *Rasbora trilineata*

Feeding

There is a wide variety of tropical fish foods available, so that it should be possible to provide an interesting and varied diet that will keep your fish in peak condition. When you put a pinch of dried food into the aquarium, you will notice that it spreads over the surface and gradually sinks when waterlogged. It is better to limit this spreading by utilising one or two floating rings that contain the food in one place. It can then be controlled and will sink over the area designated, where any food that is not immediately consumed can be easily found and removed later if still uneaten. Some fish feed at the surface, some in midwater and others scavenge from the bottom. The number of rings used must be related to the number of fish kept in order that both aggressive and non aggressive feeders each get their share. Do remember that fish are very small creatures with small appetites, and that the pollution caused from uneaten food can quickly kill them. Give only as much food as will be completely consumed in three minutes.

Dry foods These foods form the principal diet of most fish, being supplemented occasionally by frozen or live foods. Remember that dry foods lose nutritious value in proportion to the length of storage. It is better to buy supplies for a month at a time and from a shop that has a high stock turnover, to ensure freshness.

Frozen foods Brine shrimp, shrimp, sliced fish, sliced beef. Feed sparingly because they are very rich.

Live foods Earthworms, daphnia (see below), fruit flies, mosquito larvae, white worms, blood worms, algae.
   In their natural habitat, live foods would probably form a large proportion of the diet so it is reasonable to suppose that the provision of live foods makes for a more acclimatised fish, with the possibility of improved fertility and breeding performance. Some live food should form the died of all tank-bred fish.

Daphnia are very tiny water fleas that can often be found in ponds. A large, very fine net will probably get you a good supply.

Brine shrimps are an excellent food for young fish. They can be purchased as eggs, which can be easily hatched in a jar of vigorously aerated salt water at a temperature of 21.5–24 deg C (71–75 deg F). They hatch in about 24 hours.

Whiteworms can be bred in boxes filled with damp earth and peat. They are very small, segmented worms, which grow to about 2.5cm (1in) long. Although they reproduce and multiply rapidly, the culture eventually dwindles. It is better, therefore, to set up a new box in addition to the first after about four weeks, and to dispose of the first box after about 7 weeks. In this way, a constant supply can be maintained. The first culture can be purchased from an aquatic dealer.

Tubifex worms These are available from your aquatic shop, being small red worms about 2.5cm (1in) long, that are collected from the beds of rivers and streams. They should be kept fresh in a small bucket of water placed under a very slowly running tap. They should be fed to the fish in a tubifex holder, otherwise the uneaten worms can burrow down into the gravel and cause pollution.

Earthworms are an excellent food for the larger fish. Red oscars and similar fish devour even large sized worms in great gulps. Clouding of the water sometimes occurs if they are fed too frequently and care should be taken to avoid pollution.

Microworms are tiny, microscopic worms used exclusively as food for fry. Cultures are sold by aquatic dealers and they are easy to breed. Make up a small quantity of porridge, and let it thoroughly cool in a shallow dish. Add a few drops of the culture liquid, and within a few days the surface of the porridge will be teeming with thousands of minute worms. Remove them lightly with a child's paint brush, which can then be dipped into the fry tank.

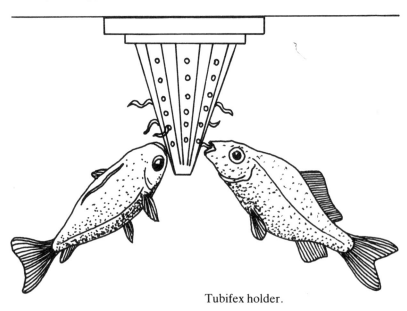

Tubifex holder.

Breeding

The breeding of tropical fish is probably the most rewarding part of fish keeping and about which many volumes have been written. The breeding habits of fish are many and varied. They can be live-bearers (viviparous), that is they give birth to live fry, or they can be egg-layers. The egg-laying (oviparous) fish can be separated into various groups; egg hiders, egg guarders, bubble nesters or egg scatterers. For the beginner, the live bearers are the easiest fish to breed. The number of fry can vary from ten to a hundred, depending on the size of the female. Some easy fish to breed are guppies, mollies and platys. When considering the large numbers of fry produced, the novice aquarist has visions of his tank becoming densely populated in a very short time but, alas, this is not so. Unfortunately, the fry make excellent food and are quickly consumed, often by their parents, unless protection is given. An apparatus designed to protect the fry can be purchased and this is known as a breeding trap. It usually consists of a small plastic container that is clipped to the inside of the tank and into which the female is placed. The base has a grille through which the fry can go but the female cannot. She is then prevented from eating them. Since the use of this device is unnatural, it cannot be recommended. It is far better to use a separate aquarium for breeding, planting it heavily to provide refuge for the newly born fish. The mother fish can be returned to the main aquarium after a day or two to recuperate, and the young fish allowed to grow in comparative safety.

A separate breeding aquarium is essential for egglayers, the bottom being covered with a shallow layer of very coarse gravel; as the eggs are laid, they fall between the grains of gravel where the parent fish cannot reach them. Some fish, like angel fish lay adhesive eggs carefully on the leaves of large plants. When the eggs hatch out, the parents watch over the fry to protect them from danger, often until they they are a month or more old.

Water temperature is very important in breeding tanks and unless you have the correct breeding temperature, and can maintain it to within a couple of degrees, you are unlikely to achieve success in breeding, even though all the other factors are ideal. A proper fish room can be a definite advantage as it permits you to have several tanks which can be maintained at varying temperatures and the results of breeding in each tank can be observed and recorded. If the outside lighting is kept very dim and the walls painted black, it serves to limit the fishs' view to within the aquarium and outside distractions are kept to a minimum. Breeders who have taken this trouble report improved results. In aquaria, spawning is not restricted to certain times of the year as in natural conditions. This is because we are able to maintain a fairly constant temperature and the seasons are indistinguishable, one from another. In some live bearers, the females may show some changes in coloration which gives an indication that spawning is about to take place. Certainly, they become much fatter due to the increase in the size of the ovaries. The males, when ready to spawn, show a more marked colour change and this acts as a visual signal to the females. Males that are ready to spawn become more aggressive towards other males that show the same breeding coloration.

When spawning takes place, the majority of species release their eggs into the water where they are fertilised by sperms from the male. After this, they are at the mercy of other fish, including the parents, who frequently consume them. Some fish species do not neglect the eggs but the male, or female, may stand guard over them until they hatch. This protection of the eggs seems to be connected with the number of eggs laid. The incidence of egg guarding is high among those species that lay eggs that are few in number. In some special cases, for example with cichlids of the genus *Haplochromis*, the eggs are sucked into the female's mouth after laying and are then fertilised. The young brood is not released until they are able to swim and they then return to their mother's mouth for protection, if needed.

In live bearers, (viviparous), the eggs are fertilised within the body and develop in the ovarian cavity. The sperms which fertilise the eggs are released by the male through the gonopodium and travel up the oviduct of the female. The young are released as free swimming fry, which are soon able to find their own food.

The size of the breeding tank has a bearing on the number of fry a fish will successfully raise and on the number of eggs that the female will lay. A large tank will produce the best results. It is in the breeding tank that the importance of getting the correct pH and hardness is most essential. Some tropical fish hobbyists have a healthy, well stocked aquarium and yet they take very little trouble to secure the right water conditions. Their tanks are none the less beautiful and their fish seem to survive, but they seldom achieve the breeding results gained by aquarists who do take the trouble to provide exactly the right water conditions. The breeding of fish is a highly complex subject, every species having its own special requirements, that are beyond the scope of this book. After deciding on the type of fish you wish to breed, you should make a thorough study of all the relevant literature available.

Discus with eggs laid on vertical glass surface.

Discus with fry on vertical plant stem.

Discus with free-swimming fry, about seven days old.

Introduction to the fish families

There are many families of freshwater fish living in the warmer parts of the world. Most of these have at least some species which are suitable for the aquarium. In this book representatives from 21 families are described, which have been chosen as being among the most suitable for aquarists. Here, there should be something for everyone: bright, lively fish; quiet, secretive fish; large specimens and small specimens; delicate, showy varieties and hardy, ever-popular varieties.

The descriptions which follow are intended to give the reader a brief introduction to each family; the fish finally chosen for your aquarium may well have characteristics which a general description cannot describe fully.

Family Anabantidae

Members of this family are also referred to as 'labyrinth' fish due to an organ in their heads which enables them to breathe air if necessary. The family is native to the waters of Africa and Asia. Members of the family originating from Asia have ventral fins modified for sensing food. These 'feelers' protrude in front of the fish to detect food in the dark waters of their natural habitat. Many members of this family produce characteristic floating bubble nests.

Family Anostomidae

The Anostomidae are a family of South American fish, many of which adopt a 'head-down' position when swimming or resting. This is thought to be a form of protective camouflage when among plants.

Family Callichthyidae

Catfish are a varied family of hardy, bottom-dwelling fish which can survive in near-stagnant water if necessary, since they have the ability to breathe atmospheric air. Some members of the family have strongly suckered mouths with which they can cling to stones, or graze algae from aquarium tank walls. Many of the most suitable tank specimens are members of the genus *Corydoras*, characterised by the possession of large, bony plates along the sides of the body. Catfish have a wide distribution in North and South America, Europe, Asia and Africa. Various egg-laying methods are adopted by the Callichthyidae.

Family Centrarchidae

The Centrarchidae is a small family of North American fish, represented in this book by the species *Elassoma evergladei*. The family is also known by the common name of sunfish. Sunfish are able to tolerate much colder water conditions than most other species.

Family Centropomidae

The members of this family are usually found in marine or brackish conditions, and those kept in aquaria thrive best in water in which a tablespoon of salt has been added to each gallon of water. Centropomids suitable for aquaria originate from Asia.

Family Characidae

Members of this family comprise one of the largest freshwater fish families in the world. This varied group ranges over Central and South America and most of Africa south of the Sahara, although the largest number of representatives come from South America. The wide variety of species means that the aquarist is sure to find specimens suitable for all types of tank. Characins are characterised by the possession of either teeth or an adipose fin, and sometimes both.

Family Cichlidae

Cichlids are territorial, mainly carnivorous fish from Asia, Africa and Central and South America. A high degree of parental protection, such as mouth-brooding, is exhibited by cichlids, which are considered to be among the more highly evolved of the fish species. Despite the aggressive reputation of the family, many species make excellent aquarium inhabitants.

Family Citharinidae

Most of the members of this African family are too large for the normal aquarium, but a few species are suitable. The Citharinidae are closely related to the Characidae.

Family Cobitidae

The Cobitidae, or loaches, are widely distributed over Europe, Asia and parts of Africa. They are bottom-dwelling fish with flattened undersides, a mouth well served with sensory barbels (or feelers) and their bodies are often armed with erectile spines – such as those situated in front of the eyes – which act as a defence mechanism. Loaches may take air from the surface, an indication that they have evolved to live in stagnant waters.

Family Cyprinidae

The Cyprinidae consist of about 1,500 species scattered throughout most of the world, and include cold water types as well as those of tropical waters. Cyprinids rely on teeth in their pharynx to break up their food. Most have sensory barbs, indicating a food-probing way of life in the bottom layers of the water. Included among the familiar cyprinid aquarium species are the barbs, rasboras, danios and minnows. The Cyprinidae are egg scatterers, preferring to disperse their eggs throughout the tank rather than relying on the burying or hanging methods favoured by other families.

Family Cyprinodontidae

This family comprises the egg-laying toothcarps or killifishes. The egg-laying toothcarps, which are found in parts of North and South America, Africa and Southern Europe and Asia, have mouths armed with teeth, which make them active predators of other, smaller species. They prefer slightly acidic water and dimly lit conditions. Two methods of egg laying are recognised: the egg-hangers lay their eggs among the roots of floating plants, and the egg-buriers (as their name suggests) prefer to bury theirs in clumps of peat or other suitable substrate material.

Family Gasteropelecidae

The hatchet fish are South American fish with characteristically shaped bodies resembling hatchets. The large, upward inclined pectoral fins are used to assist gliding when the fish jump from the water and 'fly' short distances – probably to escape danger.

Family Gobiidae

The gobies are a large family of about 600 different species ranging widely throughout the Caribbean and much of Asia. Although shy at first, gobies soon settle down and are undemanding fish, often showing interesting parental egg-guarding behaviour.

Family Hemiodontidae

The Hemiodontidae are small South American fish with slender bodies. They are often known as pencil fish. They are related to the characins, but possess teeth in the upper jaws only.

Family Monodactylidae

Also known as finger fish, the Monodactylidae are found along the coasts and estuaries of Africa, southern Asia and Australia. They prefer to live in conditions suitable for brackish water species.

Family Nandidae

Native to the waters of South America, India, Africa and parts of Asia, these are predatory, large mouthed fish with voracious appetites. The majority spawn on the bottom of the tank, with the male guarding the young.

Family Notopteridae

These are large fish with long bodies, known as knife fish. The small scales and extended anal fin give these fish an unusual appearance. Members of the family are found in both Africa and Asia.

Family Poeciliidae

The Poeciliidae, or live-bearing tooth-carps, are a family of small fish originating from the southern part of North America, Central America and northern South America. The anal fin of the male forms a sexual organ known as a gonopodium, with which sperms are introduced into the female. Live young are produced, which are capable of self-sufficient swimming and feeding minutes after they are born. Included in this family are the guppies, platys, mollies and swordtails.

Family Scatophagidae

Scats are a small family of fish found naturally in the river mouths, estuaries and coasts of south-east Asia and northern Australia. They have deep, laterally compressed bodies, two dorsal fins, and feed by scavenging on plant and animal matter. These are brackish water fish.

Family Siluridae

The Siluridae are found throughout most of central and northern Europe, and much of Asia. They are mostly bottom feeders with large sucker-like mouths. Members of this diverse family are useful additions to the aquarium, since they are undemanding and hardy, as well as serving a useful purpose by grazing algae and general tank debris.

Family Toxotidae

The Toxotidae are also known as archer fish, due to their unique method of obtaining food by squirting jets of water at insects sitting on the overhanging foliage, to knock them into the water. Archer fish are found in the coastal waters of India, Indonesia, Australia and the Persian Gulf.

KEY TO SYMBOLS

To help you identify the level at which fish prefer to swim, we have included the following symbols.

upper water   mid water   lower water   all levels

Identification guide

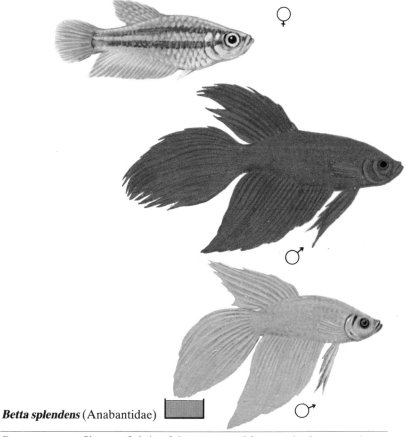

Betta splendens (Anabantidae)

Common name: Siamese fighting fish
Origin: Thailand
Size: 7.5cm (3in), females smaller
Community tank: Yes, or species tank, but aggressive and should not be mixed with males of the same species. Well-planted tank
Food: *Tubifex*, water fleas, mosquito larvae
Temperature: 25.5 – 26.5 deg C (78–80 deg F)
Breeding: Easy. Temperature 25.5–26.5 deg C (78–80 deg F). Saliva coated, floating bubble nest blown by male into which fertilised eggs are placed following nuptial embrace beneath nest. Female best removed from tank after spawning. Male guards fry, which must be safeguarded against draughts; he can be removed about 1 week after the fry become free-swimming

A beautiful, showy, active species with the male only possessing long, trailing fins. Gill covers of male raised in aggressive displays. In native country, wagers are placed on outcome of fights between males, which may bear the scars of fights, such as badly damaged fins. Many colour forms exist in this species, which prefers a small, well-planted tank.

Colisa chunae (Anabantidae)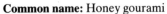

Common name: Honey gourami
Origin: India
Size: 4.5cm (1¾in)
Community tank: Yes with small, peaceful species.Provide plants as cover. Very shy
Food: *Tubifex*, dried food
Temperature: 24–26.5 deg C (75–80 deg F)
Breeding: Difficult. Temperature 28 deg C (82 deg F). Bubble nester

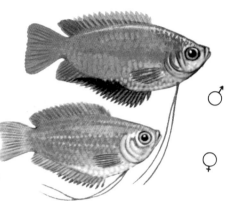

When young these fish are not particularly colourful, but the male gradually develops a rich golden-yellow colour in the dorsal fin and a salmon-pink colour over much of the body. Adult females are much less bright, with a dark stripe running along the side of the body. A peaceful fish.

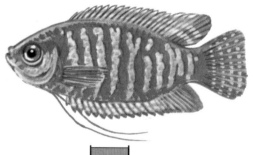

Colisa fasciata (Anabantidae)

Common name: Striped gourami
Origin: South-east Asia
Size: 11cm (4½in)
Community tank: Yes, with other medium-sized fish
Food: *Tubifex*, water fleas, dried food
Temperature: 24–26.5 deg C (75–80 deg F)
Breeding: Quite difficult. Temperature 28 deg C (82 deg F). Bubble nester

A peaceful fish, swimming at all levels in the tank. The male is by far the most brightly coloured, with a metallic blue sheen over most of the flanks, and red or orange markings on the fins and body. The female has similar markings, but less intense. Not a very active fish, so it appreciates a well-planted aquarium to give it some cover.

Colisa labiosa (Anabantidae)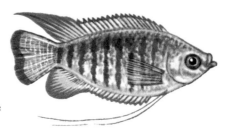

Common name: Thick-lipped gourami
Origin: Burma
Size: 7.5cm (3in)
Community tank: Yes, with some cover
Food: _Tubifex_, dried food
Temperature: 20–26.5 deg C (68–80 deg F)
Breeding: Fairly easy. Temperature 27 deg C (80 deg F). Bubble nester

One of the best gouramis for a general community aquarium, attractively coloured, not growing too large, and tolerant of a wide range of conditions and companions.

The male is by far the more brightly coloured, but in breeding condition he often turns so dark that the normal markings disappear.

Colisa lalia (Anabantidae)

Common name: Dwarf gourami
Origin: North India
Size: 5cm (2in)
Community tank: Yes, with other small, peaceful species. Provide plants as cover
Food: _Tubifex_, dried food
Temperature: 20–26.5 deg C (68–80 deg F)
Breeding: Fairly easy. Bubble nester. Temperature 26 deg C (79 deg F). Easy to breed provided you have a pair in good condition, but fry mortality is usually very high. Ensure that the fry have regular and adequate feedings of infusoria for first 3 weeks, then feed small quantities of brine shrimp as well

The male is one of the most brilliantly coloured of all tropicals, with alternating bars of metallic blue and red over the whole body: the female is much more dull. Unfortunately this fish is quite timid and spends much of the time hidden away amongst the plants whenever larger and more aggressive fish are around.

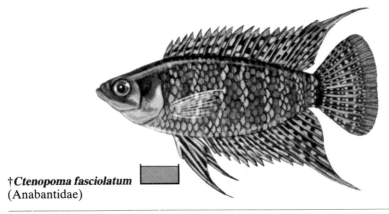

†*Ctenopoma fasciolatum*
(Anabantidae)

Common name: Banded climbing perch
Origin: Congo Basin
Size: Up to 8cm (3in)
Community tank: No
Food: Small fishes – this is a carnivorous species, worms, mosquito larvae, *Tubifex*

Temperature: 24 deg C (75 deg F)
Breeding: Not known to have bred in captivity

Climbing perches are aggressive, predatory fishes and will eat smaller fish if placed in the tank. They prefer dense vegetation in which to hide.

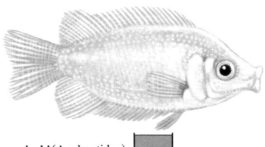

Helostoma temmincki (Anabantidae)

Common name: Kissing gourami
Origin: Borneo, Thailand, Sumatra, India
Size: 13–30cm (5–12in)
Community tank: Yes, but only with large fish
Food: *Tubifex*, water fleas, dried food, lettuce. Needs feeding well if it is to thrive
Temperature: 21–26.5 deg C (70–80 deg F)
Breeding: Temperature 29.5 deg C (85 deg F). Difficult; one of the few members of the Anabantidae which does not produce a bubble nest,

although eggs float at surface. Young fish have enormous appetites

An active fish, which can grow quite large. The 'kissing' action often seen between two fishes is probably territorial behaviour. The protruding lips are also used to scrape algae from the sides of the tank. Prefers tank with open water interspersed with robust plants. Two colour varieties are available: a dull pink variety with dark eyes; and a rarer green or yellow-silver version with striped flanks.

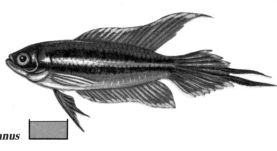

Macropodus cupanus cupanus
(Anabantidae)

Common name: Spike-tailed
paradise fish
Origin: South-east Asia
Size: Up to 7.5cm (3in)
Community tank: Yes, with
similar-sized fish
Food: *Tubifex*, water fleas, mosquito
larvae, dried food
Temperature: Moderately easy.
15–24 deg C (59–75 deg F)
Breeding: 21–25 deg C

(70–77 deg F). Males tend the
brood

This fish's common name is derived
from the shape of the tail. A very
peaceful fish which prefers a tank
with dense vegetation, and open
water for swimming. One of several
species which can tolerate slightly
lower temperatures than most
tropical fish.

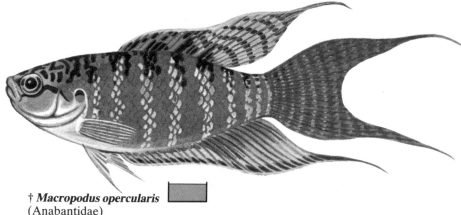

† **Macropodus opercularis**
(Anabantidae)

Common name: Paradise fish
Origin: China, Korea, Taiwan
Size: 7.5cm (3in)
Community tank: Not recommended
Food: *Tubifex*, water fleas, mosquito
larvae, earthworms, dried food
Temperature: 15–24.5 deg C
(59–76 deg F)
Breeding: Easy. Temperature 24 deg
C (75 deg F). Bubble nester

A hardy, brightly coloured fish
better kept in a species tank than in a
community tank, for it can be
aggressive to other types. Dense
vegetation with some floating plants
is preferred, together with open
water for swimming. Can tolerate
low temperatures after
acclimatization.

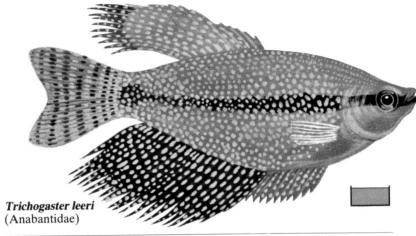

Trichogaster leeri
(Anabantidae)

Common name: Pearl gourami, Lace gourami
Origin: Thailand, Sumatra, Malaysia
Size: 10cm (4in)
Community tank: Yes, with places to hide, as a rather shy fish
Food: *Tubifex*, water fleas, mosquito larvae, dried food
Temperature: 22.5–26.5 deg C (73–80 deg F)
Breeding: Moderately easy. Temperature 26.5 deg C (80 deg F) Builds bubble nest, male looks after the young fry

When mature, the male develops a rich orange coloration over the lower front half of the body, whilst the dorsal fin becomes longer and more pointed than that of the female. When fully grown the male may occasionally chase other fish, but rarely if ever does any harm to them. The 'feelers' – actually modified ventral fins – are frequently used as sensory aids at feeding time, when approaching other fish and to examine new items placed in the aquarium.

Trichogaster trichopterus
(Anabantidae)

Common name: Three-spot gourami
Origin: Indo China, Malaysia, Burma, Indonesia
Size: 13cm (5in)
Community tank: Yes, but not with very small species
Food: *Tubifex*, water fleas, mosquito larvae, dried food
Temperature: 20–25.5 deg C (68–78 deg F)
Breeding: Temperature 26.5 deg C (80 deg F). One of the easiest of the gouramis to breed provided the pair are in good condition and of adult size. The dorsal fin of the male tapers to a point, whilst the female will be fatter in the body

with the many hundreds of eggs she is carrying. Once hatched feed heavily with infusoria and, about the second week, with brine shrimp as well

Its common name derives from the two dark spots on the body, with the eye making the third. Swims at all levels in the tank. Rather spiteful when adult.

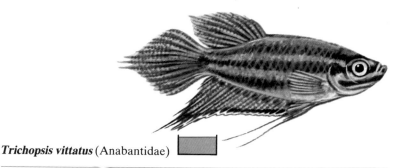

Trichopsis vittatus (Anabantidae)

Common name: Croaking gourami
Size: 5cm (2in)
Community tank: Yes, with places to hide as rather a shy fish
Food: _Tubifex_, water fleas, mosquito larvae, dried food
Temperature: 20–25.5 deg C (68–78 deg F)
Breeding: Fairly easy. Temperature 26.5 deg C (80 deg F)

Although not a brightly coloured fish, it has a slim body and long fins that give it an attractive appearance. The audible croaking noise that provides its common name is believed to be produced in the labyrinth organ. Swims at all levels in the tank.

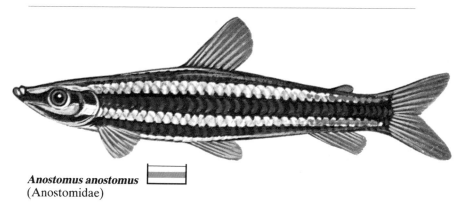

Anostomus anostomus (Anostomidae)

Common name: Striped anostomus
Origin: South America (Guyana and Amazon basin)
Size: Up to 17cm (7in)
Community tank: Yes. Peaceful when kept with similar fish and characins
Food: Small worms, water fleas, _Tubifex_, dried food
Temperature: 24–26.5 deg C (75–80 deg F)
Breeding: Not known to have bred in captivity

A very shy and timid fish despite its size. It does not swim in the manner of most other fish: instead it glides very slowly through the water, head downwards, propelled by rapid beats of its pectoral fins but the body otherwise motionless. Should it be scared it can dash rapidly to safety. Generally swims mid-water.

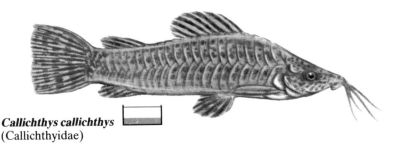

Callichthys callichthys
(Callichthyidae)

Common name: Armoured catfish
Origin: Amazon, Guyana
Size: 17cm (7in)
Community tank: Yes, even with quite small species. Lives on bottom
Food: *Tubifex*, mosquito larvae, dried food
Temperature: 19.5–25.5 deg C (67–78 deg F)
Breeding: Difficult. Bubble nester among floating plants

One of the armoured catfishes, so-called because of the heavy overlapping plates that cover the body. An excellent scavenger, but rather shy and nocturnal in its behaviour. Although not dangerous even to quite small fish, a large specimen may frighten and disturb the other occupants as it dashes to the surface for air.

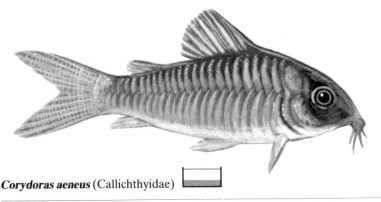

Corydoras aeneus (Callichthyidae)

Common name: Bronze corydoras
Origin: South America
Size: 7.5cm (3in)
Community tank: Yes, very peaceful. Needs to be able to reach surface for air
Food: *Tubifex*, dried food, water fleas
Temperature: 22–25.5 deg C (72–78 deg F)
Breeding: Can be bred. Temperature 25.5 deg C (78 deg F)

One of the commonest of the corydoras family. Being an excellent scavenger it is an invaluable addition to almost any aquarium. Ensure that the gravel is a smooth type otherwise its 'whiskers' will soon wear away as it forages around for food. Spends almost all its time at the bottom of the aquarium.

Corydoras hastatus (Callichthyidae)

Common name: Dwarf corydoras
Origin: South America, Amazon Basin
Size: 4.5cm (1¾in)
Community tank: Yes, with fine gravel at bottom
Food: *Tubifex*, water fleas, dried food
Temperature: 22–25.5 deg C (72–78 deg F).

Breeding: Can be bred. Temperature 26.5 deg C (80 deg F). Eggs laid on stones, hatch in 3–4 days. Parents liable to eat fry

One of the smallest of all corydoras. Unlike the other members of the family it does not spend all its time at the bottom: it often hovers in mid-water or rests on plant leaves.

Corydoras julii (Callichthyidae)

Common name: Leopard corydoras
Origin: Brazil
Size: 6cm (2½in), female larger
Community tank: Yes, excellent scavenger of uneaten food
Food: *Tubifex*, water fleas, dried food
Temperature: 22–25.5 deg C (72–78 deg F)
Breeding: Can be bred. Temperature 26.5 deg C (80 deg F)

A peaceful, bottom-living fish. This is one of the most popular of all corydoras on account of its very attractive markings and ready availability. Although initially rather shy, it soon settles down in the aquarium.

Corydoras nattereri (Callichthyidae)

Common name: Blue corydoras
Origin: Brazil
Size: 6cm (2½in), female larger
Community tank: Yes, very peaceful
Food: *Tubifex*, water fleas, mosquito larvae, dried food
Temperature: 22–25.5 deg C (72–78 deg F)

Breeding: Can be bred. Temperature 26 deg C (79 deg F)

A peaceful, bottom-living fish. The common name comes from the bluish-green sheen apparent on the flanks of mature specimens in good condition. Not commonly found.

Corydoras paleatus (Callichthyidae)

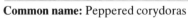

Common name: Peppered corydoras
Origin: Argentine, Brazil
Size: 7.5cm (3in)
Community tank: Yes
Food: *Tubifex*, water fleas, dried food
Temperature: 22–25.5 deg C (72–78 deg F)
Breeding: Can be bred. 24.5 deg C (76 deg F)

This is one of the largest corydoras, and therefore particularly suitable for inclusion in aquaria with large fish that might tend to disturb and worry the smaller catfish. Not as popular as it was a few years ago, perhaps because it lacks the attractive markings of some of the rarer corydoras that are now more often available. Another bottom-living species.

† *Elassoma evergladei*
(Centrarchidae)

Common name: Pygmy sunfish
Origin: Florida, North Carolina
Size: 3.5cm (1¼in)
Community tank: No, only with others of same species
Food: Water fleas, brine shrimps. algae, dried food
Temperature: 10–22 deg C (50–72 deg F)
Breeding: Moderately easy. Temperature 19 deg C (66 deg F). Builds a nest of fine leaved plants near the bottom. Eggs hatch in 48 hours

A peaceful, shy fish which prefers to establish territory. Needs a tank with dense vegetation and plenty of rockwork. This species can tolerate quite low temperatures after acclimatization.

Chanda ranga (Centropomidae)

Common name: Indian glassfish
Origin: India
Size: Up to 6cm (2½in)
Community tank: Yes, with other peaceful species
Food: *Tubifex*, water fleas – not dried food only
Temperature: 19.5–25 deg C (67–77 deg F)
Breeding: Very difficult. Temperature 24.5 deg C (76 deg F). Eggs laid among plants. Fry eat live food

An unusual, delicate, almost transparent fish which is fairly timid and likes to establish a territory in a well-planted tank. Females duller than males.

Arnoldichthys spilopterus
(Characidae)

Common name: Red eyed characin
Origin: West Africa
Size: 6cm (2½in)
Community tank: Yes, with other medium-sized fish
Food: Water fleas, earthworms, mosquito larvae, dried food
Temperature: 24–26 deg C (75–78 deg F)

Breeding: Very difficult.
Temperature 26 deg C (78 deg F)

A hardy, active fish which likes to form shoals. Prefers upper and middle water layers. Bears an adipose fin and conspicuously large scales. Male more brightly coloured than female.

Aphyocharax rubripinnis
(Characidae)

Common name: Bloodfin
Origin: Argentina
Size: Up to 5cm (2in)
Community tank: Yes
Food: _Tubifex_, water fleas, dried food
Temperature: 17–26.5 deg C (63–80 deg F)
Breeding: Difficult. When a successfully matched pair is found, spawning should take place in 15cm (6in) water at 26.5 deg C (80 deg F). Plant the aquarium heavily with fine-leaved plants, and remove parents once spawning is complete. Eggs hatch in 30–36 hours

Active, but peaceful towards other tank occupants, this little fish is happier when in a shoal. Prefers upper water layers.

Cheirodon axelrodi (Characidae)

Common name: Cardinal tetra
Origin: Rio Negro
Size: Up to 4cm (1½in)
Community tank: Yes, but keep only with peaceful species
Food: *Tubifex*, water fleas, dried food
Temperature: 22.5–25 deg C (73–77 deg F)

Breeding: Very difficult. Soft water essential if eggs are to hatch

A beautiful species which is both lively and hardy, this is a fish of the middle and lower water layers. The bright red and blue-green hues of this fish enhance any aquarium.

Copeina arnoldi (Characidae)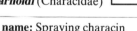

Common name: Spraying characin
Origin: Brazil, Amazon Basin
Size: 5cm (2in)
Community tank: Yes, with large leaved plants
Food: *Tubifex*, dried food
Temperature: 22–26.5 deg C (72–80 deg F)
Breeding: Difficult. Temperature 24–26.5 deg C (75–80 deg F). Lays eggs on leaves above the water surface by jumping up onto them.

Provide suitable large leaved plants. Eggs hatch after 3–4 days. The male splashes the eggs from time to time to keep them moist, by lashing the water with his tail

A fairly timid species which tends to swim among plants in the upper water layers, but well worth keeping due to its unusual breeding behaviour, and attractive appearance.

Copeina guttata (Characidae)

Common name: Red spotted copeina
Origin: Amazon
Size: 7.5cm (3in)
Community tank: Yes, with large leaved plants
Food: _Tubifex_, flies, dried food
Temperature: 22–26.5 deg C (72–80 deg F)
Breeding: Fairly easy. Temperature 24 deg C (75 deg F). Lays eggs in a depression in the sand – up to 1,000 at one spawning. The male guards the eggs, fanning them with his fins

A beautiful shoaling fish of the middle and upper water layers. The female is less colourful than the male.

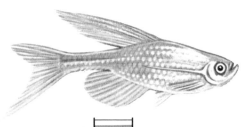

Corynopoma riisei (Characidae)

Common name: Swordtail characin
Origin: South America, West Indies, Venezuela
Size: 5cm (2in)
Community tank: Yes
Food: _Tubifex_, water fleas, dried food
Temperature: 20–25.5 deg C (68–78 deg F)
Breeding: Moderately easy. Temperature 25.5 deg C (78 deg F). Sperms of male are transferred to female's vent in a capsule. When female lays eggs they are immediately fertilised

A peaceful fish which, although not very colourful, has attractive fins. Male's fins are longer than the female's. Extremely long gill cover extensions enhance the unusual appearance.

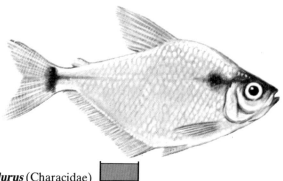

Ctenobrycon spilurus (Characidae)

Common name: Silver tetra
Origin: South America
Size: 7.5cm (3in), female larger
Community tank: Yes, but avoid keeping with long-finned fish
Food: *Tubifex*, mosquito larvae, dried food
Temperature: 20–26.5 deg C (68–80 deg F)
Breeding: Easy. Temperature 24–26.5 deg C (75–80 deg F). Lays up to 800 adhesive eggs on plants, hatching in about 48 hours

Hardy and active, but somewhat aggressive and likely to nibble the fins of other species. Should be placed in a tank with tough plants, and with open water for swimming.

Gymnocorymbus ternetzi
(Characidae)

Common name: Black widow
Origin: South America
Size: 6cm (2½in), female larger
Community tank: Yes, with fish of similar size
Food: *Tubifex*, water fleas, mosquito larvae, dried food
Temperature: 22.5–25 deg C (73–77 deg F)
Breeding: Can be bred. Temperature 26.5 deg C (80 deg F)

A shoaling fish with a tendency to lose much of its deep black coloration at maturity. This is an unusual shaped species in which the smaller male has white tail markings. A long-finned variety is also available.

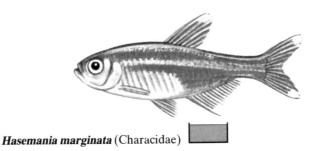

Hasemania marginata (Characidae)

Common name: Copper tetra
Origin: South America
Size: 4cm (1½in)
Community tank: Yes, preferably in a shoal
Food: _Tubifex_, water fleas, dried food
Temperature: 24 deg C (75 deg F)
Breeding: Can be bred. Egg scatterer. Fry very small and may not be seen at first

Often confused with its close relative _Hemigrammus nanus_, the Copper tetra lacks an adipose fin. A spirited little fish with a beautiful copper body colour, it takes a while to become acclimatised.

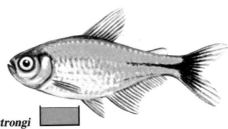

Hemigrammus armstrongi
(Characidae)

Common name: Golden tetra
Origin: Western Guyana
Size: Up to 4.5cm (1¾in)
Community tank: Yes, with some dense vegetation
Food: _Tubifex_, water fleas, dried food
Temperature: 22.5–25 deg C (73–77 deg F)

Breeding: An easily bred fish, but young bred in captivity lose their attractive golden colour

An active, shoaling species with an adipose fin. Females are stouter than males.

Hemigrammus caudovittatus
(Characidae)

Common name: Buenos Aires tetra
Origin: La Plata Basin
Size: 7.5cm (3in)
Community tank: Yes, with fish of similar size
Food: *Tubifex*, water fleas, mosquito larvae, dried food
Temperature: 22–26.5 deg C (72–80 deg F)
Breeding: Quite difficult.

Temperature 22.5 deg C (73 deg F). Lays eggs among plants

A shoaling characin with a tendency to nibble plants as well as the fins of other tank inhabitants. A rather aggressive fish, with the female of the species particularly so. Females are stouter and less colourful.

Hemigrammus erythrozonus
(Characidae)

Common name: Glowlight tetra
Origin: Guyana
Size: Up to 4.5cm (1¾in), female larger
Community tank: Yes
Food: *Tubifex*, water fleas, dried food
Temperature: 22.5–25.5 deg C (73–78 deg F)

Breeding: Moderately easy.
Temperature 26.5 deg C (80 deg F)

A brightly coloured characin of the middle water layers. Prefers a well-planted tank, but with some open water for swimming. The golden line along the body becomes brighter with age.

Hemigrammus nanus (Characidae)

Common name: Silvertips
Origin: Eastern Brazil
Size: 5cm (2in), female larger
Community tank: Yes, preferably in a shoal
Food: _Tubifex_, water fleas, dried food

Temperature: 24 deg C (75 deg F)
Breeding: Difficult. Egg scatterer

A lively fish, often confused with _Hasemania marginata_ from which it differs by having an adipose fin.

Hemigrammus ocellifer (Characidae)

Common name: Beacon, Head-and-tail light
Origin: Amazon Basin, Guyana
Size: 5cm (2in)
Community tank: Yes, peaceful with fish of similar size
Food: _Tubifex_, water fleas, dried food
Temperature: 22–26.5 deg C (72–80 deg F)
Breeding: Moderately easy.

Temperature 24 deg C (75 deg F). Egg scatterer

Another active characin, which likes to form shoals. The dorsal fin is set well back along the top of the body, and the tail is partly covered in scales. The name head-and-tail light fish comes from the golden spots visible in the eye and tail base.

Hemigrammus rhodostomus
(Characidae)

Common name: Red nosed tetra, Rummy nosed tetra
Origin: Lower Amazon
Size: 4cm (1½in), female larger
Community tank: Yes
Food: *Tubifex*, water fleas, dried food
Temperature: 22.5–25 deg C (73–77 deg F)
Breeding: Moderately easy. Large well planted tank required, 25cm (10in) deep

An attractive species, best viewed in a softly lit tank. Tends to form shoals in the middle water layers. The male's anal fin bears tiny hooks – beware of these catching on nets if removing the fish from the water.

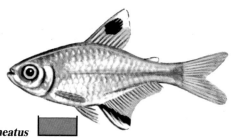

Hemigrammus unilineatus
(Characidae)

Common name: Feather-fin
Origin: South America
Size: 6cm (2½in), female larger
Community tank: Yes, with some dense vegetation
Food: *Tubifex*, water fleas, dried food
Temperature: 20–25 deg C (68–77 deg F)
Breeding: Moderately easy. Temperature 24–25 deg C (75–77 deg F)

A shy, retiring characin which tends to prefer to stay close to its chosen spot in the aquarium. Very peaceful.

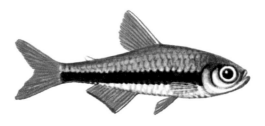

Hyphessobrycon eos (Characidae)

Common name: Dawn tetra
Origin: Guyana
Size: 5cm (2in)
Community tank: Yes
Food: Water fleas, mosquito larvae, dried food
Temperature: 24 deg C (75 deg F)
Breeding: Not easy to breed in captivity

A beautiful little fish with bold markings. The males and females show no external differences. Prefers to swim in the middle layers of a well-planted tank.

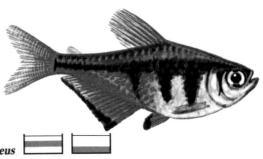

Hyphessobrycon flammeus
(Characidae)

Common name: Flame tetra
Origin: South America
Size: 4cm (1½in), female a little larger
Community tank: Yes, with some dense vegetation
Food: _Tubifex_, water fleas, dried food
Temperature: 20–25 deg C (68–77 deg F)

Breeding: Easy. Temperature 22–24 deg C (72–75 deg F). Eggs laid among plants, hatch in 48 hours

A peaceful and beautiful fish, but seldom seen with the brilliant colours it should possess. The female is duller, and larger. Prefers middle and lower water layers.

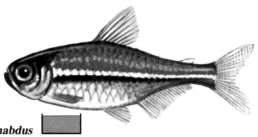

Hyphessobrycon heterorhabdus
(Characidae)

Common name: Flag tetra
Origin: Amazon
Size: 5cm (2in), female larger
Community tank: Yes, with similar sized fish
Food: *Tubifex*, water fleas, dried food
Temperature: 22.5–25 deg C (73–77 deg F)

Breeding: Difficult

A lively but placid shoaling fish with a blunt nose, which prefers a well-planted tank with some open water for swimming. Females are larger and stouter.

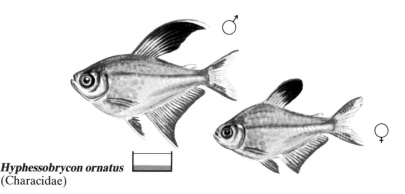

Hyphessobrycon ornatus
(Characidae)

Origin: South America
Size: 4cm (1½in)
Community tank: Yes
Food: *Tubifex*, water fleas, dried food
Temperature: 22.5–25.5 deg C (73–78 deg F)
Breeding: Moderately easy. Temperature 26.5 deg C (80 deg F)

A hardy characin which prefers the bottom layers of the tank, where it forms peaceful shoals. Males are smaller, but possess larger dorsal fins.

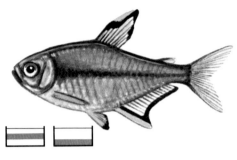

Hyphessobrycon pulchripinnis
(Characidae)

Common name: Lemon tetra
Origin: Amazon Basin
Size: 4cm (1½in)
Community tank: Yes
Food: _Tubifex_, water fleas, dried food
Temperature: 22.5–25 deg C (73–77 deg F)
Breeding: Fairly easy. Temperature 26.5 deg C (80 deg F)

A peaceful fish of the middle and lower water layers. Likes to form shoals and, if threatened, to retreat to a favourite hiding place. A delicate lemon-yellow coloured fish to grace any aquarium.

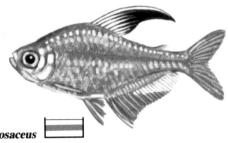

Hyphessobrycon rosaceus
(Characidae)

Common name: Rosy tetra
Origin: Guyana and Brazil
Size: 4.5cm (1¾in)
Community tank: Yes, with other small fish
Food: _Tubifex_, water fleas, dried food
Temperature: 24.5 deg C (76 deg F)

Breeding: Moderately difficult. Temperature 26.5 deg C (80 deg F)

An elegant fish, ideal for the community tank, being peaceful and possessing strong body coloration. The males have rather longer finnage, and brighter markings.

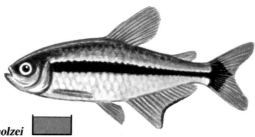

Hyphessobrycon scholzei
(Characidae)

Common name: Black-line tetra
Origin: Amazon
Size: 5cm (2in)
Community tank: Yes
Food: *Tubifex*, water fleas, dried food
Temperature: 22–25 deg C (72–77 deg F)

Breeding: Easy. Temperature 25.5 deg C (78 deg F)

An attractive shoaling fish with a peaceful nature. Prefers dense vegetation in which to hide, and open water for swimming.

Hyphessobrycon serpae
(Characidae)

Common name: Blood characin, Serpae tetra
Origin: South America (Amazon, Madeira, Paraguay)
Size: Up to 6cm (2½in)
Community tank: No, keep with same species
Food: *Tubifex*, water fleas, dried food
Temperature: 24 deg C (75 deg F)
Breeding: Moderately easy. Temperature 25.5 deg C (78 deg F).

Egg scatterer. Fry hatch within 24 hours, and cling to tank sides for about 3 days, after which they become free-swimming

This fish derives its name from its deep red body and fins, tinged with black. It has a reputation as a fin nipper. Males are smaller, more colourful and have more elaborate fin patterns.

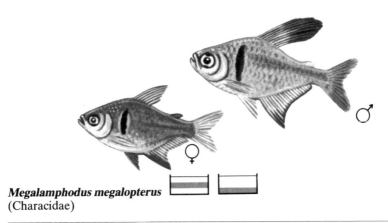

Megalamphodus megalopterus
(Characidae)

Common name: Phantom tetra
Origin: Brazil
Size: 4cm (1½in)
Community tank: Yes, but not in too bright a light
Food: *Tubifex*, mosquito larvae, dried food
Temperature: 22.5–25.5 deg C (73–78 deg F)

Breeding: Can be bred

A pretty and hardy fish with a peaceful nature. This fish prefers the lower and middle water layers of well-planted tanks. The dorsal fin of the male becomes long and flowing with age.

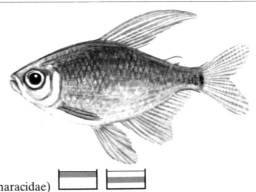

Moenkhausia pittieri (Characidae)

Common name: Diamond tetra
Origin: Venezuela (Lake Valencia)
Size: 6cm (2½in)
Community tank: Yes
Food: *Tubifex*, mosquito larvae, dried food
Temperature: 22–25.5 deg C (72–78 deg F)
Breeding: Difficult. Temperature 25.5 deg C (78 deg F)

An elegant and active shoaling characin of the middle and upper water layers. This fish is characterised by the possession of an adipose fin. Dense vegetation with open water for swimming is preferred.

Nematobrycon palmeri (Characidae)

Common name: Emperor tetra
Origin: Colombia
Size: 5cm (2in)
Community tank: Yes
Food: *Tubifex*, water fleas, mosquito larvae, dried food
Temperature: 25 deg C (77 deg F)
Breeding: Temperature 26.5 deg C (80 deg F). Although not very difficult to spawn, this is not a very prolific breeder

Emperor tetras are among the most popular freshwater fish kept by aquarists. A lively but peaceful shoaling species of the lower waters. The males do, however, threaten each other, but without serious consequences.

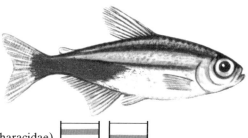

Paracheirodon innesi (Characidae)

Common name: Neon tetra
Origin: Amazon
Size: 4cm (1½in)
Community tank: Yes, with fish of similar size
Food: *Tubifex*, dried food
Temperature: 20–25 deg C (68–77 deg F)
Breeding: Difficult. Temperature 24 deg C (75 deg F). Very soft water

A beautiful fish which will enhance any aquarium. Its other merits are its peaceful nature and hardiness. Prefers middle and lower water layers in tank with dense vegetation and open water for swimming.

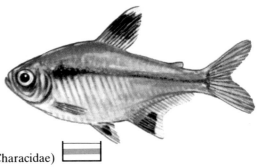

Pristella riddlei (Characidae)

Common name: X-ray fish
Origin: South America
Size: 5cm (2in), female larger
Community tank: Yes, but not too much light
Food: *Tubifex*, water fleas, dried food
Temperature: 20–25.5 deg C (68–78 deg F)
Breeding: Fairly easy. Temperature 26.5 deg C (80 deg F). Fry hatch in 24 hours. An easy characin to breed, but an avid egg eater

The name X-ray fish is derived from the fact that the fish's internal organs can be seen inside its body. A peaceful and hardy shoaling fish preferring a sparsely planted tank.

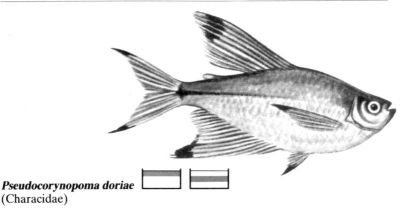

Pseudocorynopoma doriae (Characidae)

Common name: Dragon finned characin
Origin: South America (Brazil and La Plata)
Size: 8cm (3in)
Community tank: Yes
Food: Water fleas, *Tubifex* and dried food
Temperature: 24 deg C (75 deg F)
Breeding: Moderately easy. Temperature 26 deg C (79 deg F)

A very undemanding and hardy fish of the middle and upper water layers. A species not often available, it has a gleaming silver translucent body.

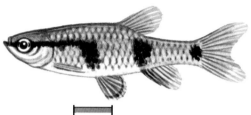

Pyrrhulina vittata (Characidae)

Common name: Striped pyrrhulina
Origin: South America
Size: 5cm (2in)
Community tank: Yes
Food: Water fleas, *Tubifex* and dried larvae, dried food
Temperature: 24 deg C (75 deg F)
Breeding: Can be bred. Eggs deposited on leaves which are first carefully cleaned and guarded by male

A peaceful fish of the upper water layers, with an elongated golden-brown body and colourful fins. A pretty little fish with interesting breeding behaviour.

Thayeria obliqua (Characidae)

Common name: Penguin fish
Origin: Amazon Basin
Size: 7.5cm (3in)
Community tank: Yes. Aquarium should be covered at all times, as this is a very active leaping fish
Food: *Tubifex*, water fleas, mosquito larvae, dried food
Temperature: 22.5–26.5 deg C (73–80 deg F)
Breeding: Moderately easy. Eggs deposited on lower leaves of plants, hatch in about 48 hours. Fry need to free on algae

A common characin which swims in a characteristic 'tail-down' position. Active, but peaceful, this fish prefers a well-planted tank, with open water for swimming.

59

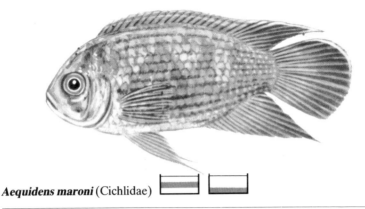

Aequidens maroni (Cichlidae)

Common name: Keyhole cichlid
Origin: Venezuela, Guyana
Size: 10cm (4in)
Community tank: Yes, with other medium-sized fish. Peaceful, but choose strong rooting plants as cichlids are liable to uproot them
Food: Earthworms, mosquito larvae, water fleas, *Tubifex*, may take dry food
Temperature: 22–25 deg C (72–77 deg F)

Breeding: Fairly easy. Temperature 26.5 deg C (80 deg F). Large aquarium preferred

A very chunky-bodied fish, but a peaceful one. Its common name comes from the keyhole-shaped dark patch that adorns the rear part of the body, though this may become less pronounced as the fish gets older. A heavy feeder, and good filtration is necessary.

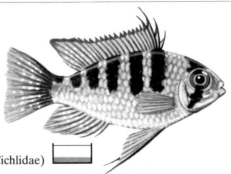

Apistogramma ramirezi (Cichlidae)

Common name: Ramirez's dwarf cichlid, Ram
Origin: Venezuela
Size: 5cm (2in)
Community tank: Yes, with some dense vegetation
Food: Water fleas, mosquito larvae, *Tubifex*. May accept dried food
Temperature: 24.5–25.5 deg C (76–78 deg F)
Breeding: Difficult Temperature 28 deg C (83 deg F)

The male is probably the prettiest of all the dwarf cichlids, but this is one of the more difficult of that group to keep. It does best in water that is rather soft and acid, and newly introduced specimens may not acclimatise well to their new home, and will often have to be tempted with various live foods. Fairly peaceful, it spends its time near the bottom of the aquarium.

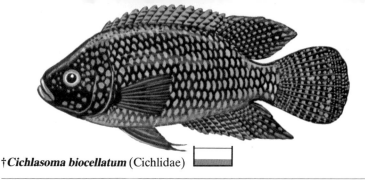

†*Cichlasoma biocellatum* (Cichlidae)

Common name: Jack Dempsey
Origin: South America
Size: 17cm (6¾in)
Community tank: No, very aggressive
Food: *Tubifex*, water fleas, earthworms, chopped meat, fishes, dried food
Temperature: 20–25 deg C (68–77 deg F)
Breeding: Easy. Temperature 25 deg C (77 deg F). Adhesive eggs deposited on stones

One of the larger cichlids, and one of the most brilliantly coloured with metallic blue spangles over a dark-coloured body. Its common name, honouring a great boxing champion, is a particularly accurate guide to its own belligerent behaviour. A specialist fish of the lower levels needing plenty of space.

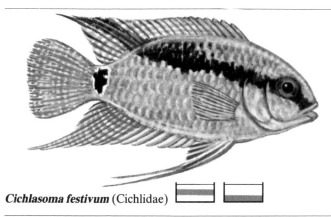

Cichlasoma festivum (Cichlidae)

Common name: Festivum
Origin: Amazon, Guyana
Size: 15cm (6in), male larger
Community tank: Yes, in a roomy tank with other medium-sized fishes. Timid and peaceful, requires hiding places
Food: *Tubifex*, water fleas, earthworms
Temperature: 20–25 deg C (68–77 deg F)
Breeding: Fairly easy. Temperature 25 deg C (77 deg F). Eggs deposited on stones

One of the most peaceful, even shy, of all cichlids despite its size. It prefers the middle and lower water layers. Although not brightly coloured, the bold diagonal line running from dorsal fin down through the eye gives the fish an imposing appearance.

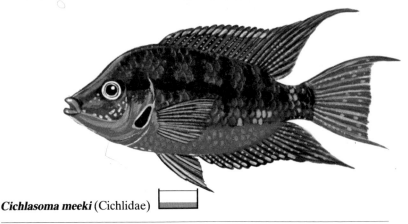

Cichlasoma meeki (Cichlidae)

Common name: Firemouth cichlid
Origin: Yucatan, Guatemala
Size: Up to 15cm (6in), female smaller
Community tank: May be kept in a large tank with different species: two males will fight.
Food: *Tubifex*, water fleas, mosquito larvae, dried foods
Temperature: 20–25 deg C (68–77 deg F)

Breeding: Easy. Temperature 25.5 deg C (78 deg F)

When young, this fish has an unattractive olive coloured body, but as it matures the belly turns to a deep red, heightened still further at breeding time. Relatively peaceful, it prefers the lower layers, but it may dig up the plants and rearrange the gravel at breeding time.

†***Cichlasoma nigrofasciatum*** (Cichlidae)

Common name: Zebra cichlid
Origin: Central and South America
Size: Up to 10cm (4in)
Community tank: No, aggressive. Also eats or uproots the plants
Food: *Tubifex*, earthworms, chopped meat
Temperature: 20–26.5 deg C (68–80 deg F)
Breeding: Very easy if you have a compatible pair. Temperature 25 deg C (77 deg F). Builds nest in gravel amongst rocks. Very prolific

Although only a small-growing cichlid, this is one of the most destructive members of the family, both in its attacks on other fish and its assaults on the aquarium furnishings.

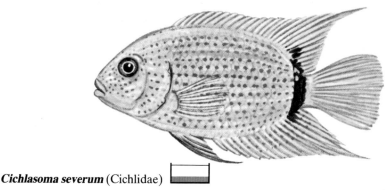

Cichlasoma severum (Cichlidae)

Common name: Banded cichlid
Origin: South America, Guyana
Size: 17cm (6¾in)
Community tank: Yes, with other large fish, in a large aquarium
Food: *Tubifex*, earthworms, chopped meat, fishes, dried food
Temperature: 22–26.5 deg C (72–80 deg F)
Breeding: Moderately easy. Temperature 26.5 deg C (80 deg F)

Many years ago this fish was known as the 'poor man's discus', which it resembles somewhat in shape. It is a good community fish with others of a similar size but needs plenty of space and a refuge of rockwork that it can regard as its own territory. A relatively peaceful fish of the lower layers.

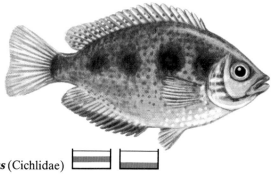

Etroplus maculatus (Cichlidae)

Common name: Orange chromide
Origin: India and Sri Lanka
Size: 7.5cm (3in)
Community tank: Yes, amongst medium-sized fish and with plenty of shelter
Food: *Tubifex*, water fleas, whiteworms, aquatic insects, dried food
Temperature: 20–25.5 deg C (68–78 deg F)

Breeding: Moderately easy. Temperature 26.5 deg C (80 deg F)

Not a very commonly found cichlid, but one that is rarely agressive amongst medium-sized fish except at breeding time. Less destructive with plants than most cichlids, it swims in the middle and lower water layers.

Haplochromis multicolor (Cichlidae)

Common name: Egyptian mouthbrooder
Origin: Egypt, East Africa
Size: 7.5cm (3in)
Community tank: Yes, with medium-sized fish.
Although small, quite aggressive. Needs places to hide
Food: *Tubifex*, water fleas, earthworms, chopped meat, dried foods
Temperature: 20–25 deg C (68–77 deg F)
Breeding: Temperature 25 deg C (77 deg F). Eggs are laid in usual cichlid manner in a depression in the gravel, but are then incubated in the female's mouth. Even when they hatch out, the fry remain in the female's mouth for much of the time, using it as a refuge from danger. By about the third week they are large enough to look after themselves, and the by now much-thinner female will start to feed normally again

Although not a very popular fish, it makes an interesting occupant for a large community aquarium well-furnished with plants and rocks. Strongly territorial in the lower layers of the tank, so better with fish other than cichlids.

† **Hemichromis bimaculatus** (Cichlidae)

Common name: Jewel cichlid
Origin: Africa
Size: 13cm (5in)
Community tank: No, a very aggressive fish. Keep only as a pair, and with plenty of rocks to provide cover
Food: *Tubifex,* mosquito larvae, small earthworms
Temperature: 24 deg C (75 deg F)
Breeding: Temperature 25 deg C (77 deg F), medium-hard water. Easy to breed provided you have a mature and compatible pair. The youngsters will grow rapidly, and need plenty of space if they are to thrive

The male, in breeding condition, is a beautiful creature with brilliant red and blue spangles all over the body. Unfortunately it is so aggressive that it will rarely live with even its own kind, so it really is a fish for the specialist. A fish of the lower layers.

Nannacara anomala (Cichlidae)

Common name: Golden-eyed dwarf cichlid
Origin: Guyana
Size: 7cm (2¾in), male larger
Community tank: Yes, with other dwarf cichlids in well-planted tank. Prefers middle and lower water layers
Food: *Tubifex*, water fleas, mosquito larvae, dried food
Temperature: 22–26.5 deg C (72–80 deg F)
Breeding: Temperature 26.5 deg C (80 deg F). This is one of the few species of fish that can actually be bred in a community aquarium, thanks to the care that the parents take of the eggs and subsequently the fry. A large aquarium is recommended, with plenty of plants and clumps of rocks to provide a spawning site for the parents. Does best with other dwarf cichlids.

A rather secretive fish, tending to stay at the lower levels of the aquarium. Not generally aggressive other than at breeding time.

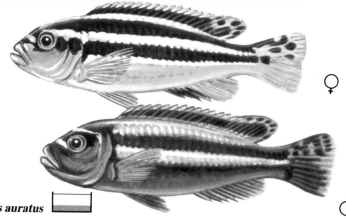

♀

♂

†Pseudotropheus auratus
(Cichlidae)

Origin: Lake Nyasa, Africa
Size: 10cm (4in), male larger
Community tank: No. Male is aggressive to female. Cover should be provided. Initially, male and female should be separated by glass partition until acclimatised.
Food: *Tubifex*, water fleas, mosquito larvae, earthworms, dried food
Temperature: 22–25 deg C (72–77 deg F)
Breeding: Temperature 24 deg C (75 deg F). The female incubates the young in her mouth, and guards them from other occupants in the aquarium. In breeding condition the male turns from a yellow coloration to a very dark blue/black.

This is one of the most common and hardy of the cichlids coming from the African Rift Valley lakes, and also one of the prettiest. Unfortunately its aggressive behaviour makes it a specialist's fish. It prefers lower water layers.

Pterophyllum scalare (Cichlidae)

Common name: Angel fish
Origin: Amazon
Size: 13cm (5in)
Community tank: Yes, while small.
When full grown may become
aggressive towards smaller fish
Food: *Tubifex*, water fleas, dried
food
Temperature: 22–26.5 deg C
(72–80 deg F)
Breeding: Moderately easy.
Temperature 26.5 deg C (80 deg F).
Up to 1,000 eggs laid on rocks over a
small area, during a 2 hour spawning
period. The female fans the eggs
while the male stands guard

One of the most graceful of
aquarium fish and especially
beautiful when large, but some
specimens can bully other
slow-swimming or long-finned fish.
Becomes quite tame after a while,
recognizing its owner's approach at
feeding time. Regular feeding with
live foods is recommended. Swims at
all levels in the aquarium.

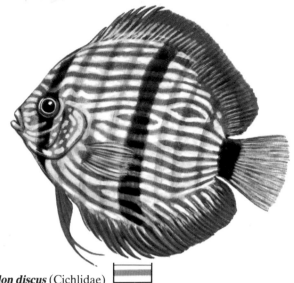

†*Symphysodon discus* (Cichlidae)

Common name: Discus
Origin: Amazon
Size: 14cm (5½in)
Community tank: No, species tank with large plants and dense vegetation. Not for beginners
Food: *Tubifex*, water fleas, mosquito larvae. Varied as much as possible
Temperature: 24–26.5 deg C (75–80 deg F)
Breeding: Very difficult. Temperature 29 deg C (84 deg F), water slightly acid and soft. The parents lay the eggs on a large leaf or piece of slate. The eggs hatch after about 3 days, and the fry feed on a special mucus secreted by the parents for the first few weeks

This is one of the most striking of all tropical fish when adult, but needs plenty of space and little disturbance if it is to thrive. Young specimens are often of poor quality, and refuse to feed which leads to their eventual death. Prefers the middle layers.

Nannaethiops unitaeniatus (Citharinidae)

Common name: One-striped African characin
Origin: Central Africa
Size: Males 6cm (2½in), females 7.5cm (3in)
Community tank: Yes
Food: *Tubifex*, water fleas, dried food
Temperature: 22–26.5 deg C (72–80 deg F)
Breeding: Temperature 25.5–26.5 deg C (78–80 deg F). Ready breeder, depositing eggs among fine leaved plants. Eggs hatch in 48 hours

A shy, but attractive fish which can be induced out of hiding by offering live food. Females deeper in the body than males. Should be kept with fish of a similar size, or smaller.

Acanthopthalmus semicinctus
(Cobitidae)

Common name: Half-banded coolie loach
Origin: Malay Archipelago
Size: 7.5cm (3in)
Community tank: Yes. Ensure it does not get trapped in filter pipes
Food: *Tubifex*, daphnia, dried food
Temperature: 24–26.5 deg C (75–80 deg F)
Breeding: Has occurred in community aquaria with large amount of rockwork to provide shelter

A peaceful bottom-dwelling loach, with an interesting body pattern, preferring to remain hidden by day but active at night. Likes plenty of rockwork with coves and plants, where it searches for food with its sensory barbels.

Botia macracanthus (Cobitidae)

Common name: Clown loach
Origin: Sumatra, Borneo
Size: Up to 30cm (12in) in wild, 10cm (4in) in captivity
Community tank: Yes, with medium-sized fish, or species tank. Sensitive to chemicals in water
Food: *Tubifex*, water fleas, mosquito larvae
Temperature: 24–26.5 deg C (75–80 deg F)
Breeding: Not known to have bred in captivity

Less shy than some of the loaches, this bottom-dwelling species is active both by day and night. Prefers a tank with rocks and roots which give cover. Its bright coloration makes it one of the favourite loaches.

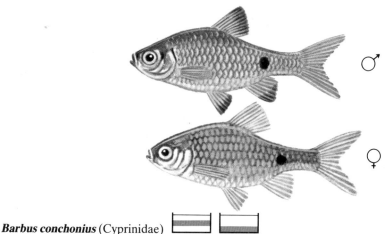

Barbus conchonius (Cyprinidae)

Common name: Rosy barb
Origin: India
Size: Up to 9cm (3½in)
Community tank: Yes, with plenty of open water for swimming
Food: *Tubifex*, water fleas, mosquito larvae, dried food
Temperature: 22–25 deg C (72–77 deg F)
Breeding: Easy. Temperature 24 deg C (75 deg F). The male becomes a bright red colour at spawning time. Parents must be separated from eggs immediately after spawning otherwise they will eat the eggs

Hardy species lacking barbels, which can live for 3 years or more. Females stouter than males, and coloured a rather drab olive-green.

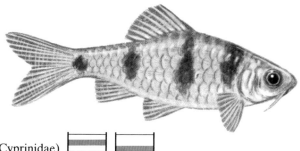

Barbus everetti (Cyprinidae)

Common name: Clown barb
Origin: South-east Asia (Singapore, Sarawak, Borneo)
Size: Up to 12cm (5in), female larger
Community tank: Yes, with large fish
Food: *Tubifex*, water fleas, dried food
Temperature: 25–26.5 deg C (77–80 deg F)
Breeding: Difficult. Temperature 26.5 deg C (80 deg F). Very prolific when spawning does occur

A large, colourful barb which prefers the middle and lower waters. An active fish, so do not plant the aquarium too fully.

69

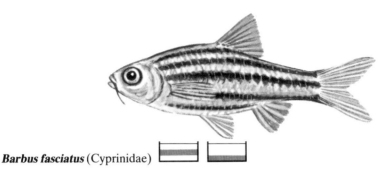

Barbus fasciatus (Cyprinidae)

Common name: Striped barb; Zebra
barb
Origin: South-east Asia
Size: 12cm (5in), female larger
Community tank: Yes
Food: *Tubifex*, mosquito larvae,
dried food
Temperature: 20–25.5 deg C
(68–78 deg F)
Breeding: Difficult. Temperature
25.5 deg C (78 deg F)

Less popular variety than most other
barbs, owing to larger size. A
shoaling fish which prefers lower and
middle water layers.

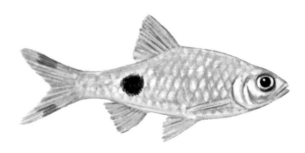

Barbus filamentosus (Cyprinidae)

Common name: Black-spot barb
Origin: South-east Asia
Size: 15cm (6in)
Community tank: Yes, with
similar-sized fish
Food: *Tubifex*, water fleas, mosquito
larvae, dried food, lettuce
Temperature: 17–25 deg C
(63–77 deg F)

Breeding: Fairly easy. Large tank
required. Over 1,000 eggs may be
spawned at one time

Peaceful and hardy. A shoaling fish
of middle and lower water layers.
When immature, this fish has black
bars on the body which resemble
those of a tiger barb.

Barbus gelius (Cyprinidae)

Common name: Golden dwarf barb
Origin: India
Size: 4cm (1½in)
Community tank: Yes, but keep with fishes of similar size and peaceful disposition
Food: *Tubifex*, water fleas, dried food
Temperature: 20–26.5 deg C (68–80 deg F)
Breeding: Moderately easy. Temperature 26.5 deg C (80 deg F). With plenty of spawning material available, a pair can be induced to lay about 100 eggs. Parents will quickly eat their eggs so they should be separated from them as soon as possible. Eggs hatch in 24 hours. Fry very quickly hide after hatching

One of the smallest of the barbs, and less popular than others, possibly due to its less striking body colours. However, the subtle golden hues and undemanding nature of this little fish can make it a useful choice for the smaller tank.

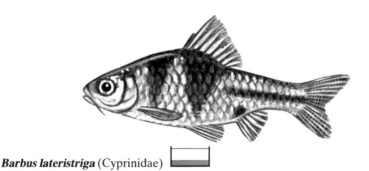

Barbus lateristriga (Cyprinidae)

Common name: Spanner barb
Origin: South-east Asia (Malay Peninsula, Singapore)
Size: 15cm (6in)
Community tank: Yes, with other medium-sized fish.
Food: *Tubifex*, water fleas, mosquito larvae, dried food
Temperature: 21–25 deg C (70–77 deg F)

Breeding: Difficult. Temperature 24–26.5 deg C (75–80 deg F).

A peaceful and hardy barb, preferring to live near the bottom. Has 2 pairs of sensory barbels. Sexing is difficult, but females have a deeper body than males. Needs a large aquarium.

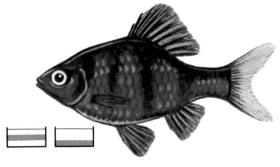

Barbus nigrofasciatus
(Cyprinidae)

Common name: Ruby barb, Nigger barb
Origin: Sri Lanka
Size: 6cm (2½in)
Community tank: Yes, with plenty of open water for swimming
Food: *Tubifex*, water fleas, mosquito larvae, dried food
Temperature: 20–26.5 deg C (68–80 deg F)
Breeding: Fairly easy. Temperature 24 deg C (75 deg F)

Shoaling barb of middle and lower waters. Characterised by a lack of sensory barbels. Likes a well-planted tank, but with open water for swimming. A firm favourite, with the males being more brightly coloured than the females. Two or more males in a tank will produce beautiful body hues as they show off to each other.

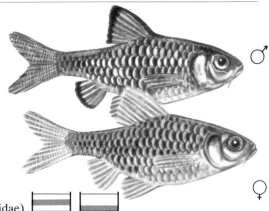

Barbus oligolepis (Cyprinidae)

Common name: Checker barb
Origin: Sumatra
Size: 5cm (2in)
Community tank: Yes, colourful and peaceful
Food: *Tubifex*, mosquito larvae, dried food
Temperature: 20–25 deg C (68–77 deg F)
Breeding: Difficult. Temperature 26 deg C (79 deg F), Spawning can be attempted when males begin showing off to each other

Active, shoaling barb with the male of the species being more brightly coloured than the female: the male's dorsal fin is edged with a black line. Possesses one pair of sensory barbels. One of the most peaceful barbs, even when kept with very small fish.

Barbus schuberti (Cyprinidae)

Common name: Golden barb, Schubert's barb
Origin: Unknown
Size: 7.5cm (3in), female larger
Community tank: Yes
Food: *Tubifex*, mosquito larvae, dried food
Temperature: 20–25 deg C (68–77 deg F)
Breeding: Fairly easy. Requires conditions similar to most other barbs

The exact origin of this fish is unknown, although it is believed to have been bred from a strain of *B. semifasciolatus*. Males have a row of black spots on the body which are absent in females. Prefers middle and lower water layers, where it forms peaceful shoals.

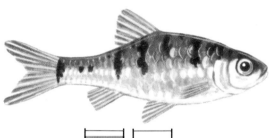

Barbus semifasciolatus (Cyprinidae)

Common name: Half-banded barb
Origin: China
Size: 6cm (2½in), female larger
Community tank: Yes
Food: *Tubifex*, water fleas, mosquito larvae, dried food
Temperature: 18–25 deg C (64–77 deg F)
Breeding: Easy. Temperature 24 deg C (75 deg F). An avid egg eater which should be separated from eggs after spawning

A peaceful, shoaling barb of middle and lower water layers, characterised by the possession of very small sensory barbels. Males are slimmer than females. One of only a few aquarium fish of Chinese origin, and one which can withstand quite low water temperatures after acclimatisation.

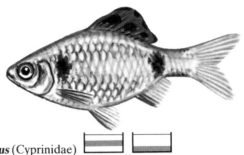

Barbus stoliczkanus (Cyprinidae)

Common name: Stoliczka's barb
Origin: Burma
Size: 6cm (2½in)
Community tank: Yes
Food: *Tubifex*, water fleas, mosquito larvae, dried food
Temperature: 19–25 deg C (66–77 deg F)
Breeding: Easy. Temperature 24–26 deg C (75–79 deg F). 300–400 eggs produced. Fry are greedy eaters

This beautiful, hardy fish has no sensory barbels and prefers to live in the middle and lower water layers where it forms shoals. A well-planted tank with open water for swimming is preferred.

Barbus tetrazona (Cyprinidae)

Common name: Tiger barb, Sumatra barb
Origin: Malay Peninsula, Borneo, Thailand, Sumatra
Size: Up to 5cm (2in), female larger
Community tank: Yes. A good shoaling fish
Food: *Tubifex*, water fleas, mosquito larvae, dried food
Temperature: 20–25 deg C (68–77 deg F)
Breeding: Can be bred. Temperature 26.5 deg C (80 deg F)

The tiger barb is perhaps the most popular of all the barbs, being an active swimmer in the middle layers. Shoals display a distinct hierarchy and 'pecking order'. This fish sometimes has a reputation as a bully, and fin nipping of other species may occur.

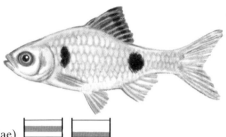

Barbus ticto (Cyprinidae)

Common name: Ticto barb, Two-spot barb
Origin: India, Sri Lanka
Size: 6cm (2½in)
Community tank: Yes
Food: *Tubifex*, water fleas, mosquito larvae, dried food
Temperature: 20–25 deg C (68–77 deg F)
Breeding: Can be bred. Temperature 24–26 deg C (75–79 deg F). Males show an overall red colour on their bodies when in breeding condition

A fish with a lively nature, preferring middle and lower water layers. The alternative name of two-spot barb is apparent from the two dark marks on the side of the body.

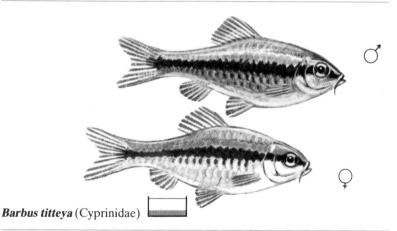

♂

♀

Barbus titteya (Cyprinidae)

Common name: Cherry barb
Origin: Sri Lanka
Size: 5cm (2in)
Community tank: Yes
Food: *Tubifex*, water fleas, mosquito larvae
Temperature: 22.5–25.5 deg C (73–78 deg F)
Breeding: Can be bred. Temperature 25.5 deg C (78 deg F), eggs hatch in about 40 hours. Vigorous males display actively, and should be placed with 2 females at breeding time

Another favourite barb, with the bright cherry coloration of breeding males being renowned. Hardy and active, yet peaceful to other tank occupants, this fish favours lower water layers.

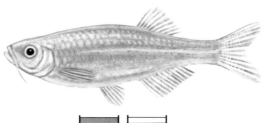

Brachydanio albolineatus
(Cyprinidae)

Common name: Pearl danio
Origin: Burma, India, Malaya
Size: 6cm (2½in), male smaller
Community tank: Yes
Food: Water fleas, dried food
Temperature: 20–25 deg C (68–77 deg F)
Breeding: Easy. Temperature 24–25.5 deg C (75–78 deg F). Eggs hatch in 48 hours

An active, pretty fish which prefers upper and middle water layers. Females stouter than males (best viewed from above). These fish are best kept in tanks with good lighting, to show their colours most effectively. A golden variety is also available.

Brachydanio frankei (Cyprinidae)

Common name: Leopard danio
Origin: India
Size: 5cm (2in)
Community tank: Yes
Food: Water fleas, dried food
Temperature: 20–25 deg C (68–77 deg F)
Breeding: Easy. Temperature 25 deg C (77 deg F)

An active fish with pretty 'leopard' markings, benefiting from a tank with good lighting. Two pairs of barbels present. A shoaling fish which prefers upper and middle layers. Females stouter than males.

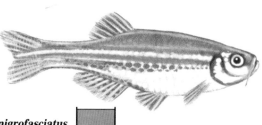

Brachydanio nigrofasciatus
(Cyprinidae)

Common name: Spotted danio
Origin: Burma
Size: 5cm (2in)
Community tank: Yes
Food: Water fleas, dried food
Temperature: 18–25 deg C (64–77 deg F)
Breeding: Easy. Eggs are non-adhesive, and readily eaten by female. Eggs hatch in 48 hours

Delightful little fish with an interesting pattern of colouring. The female is stouter than the male in this hardy species, which prefers tanks with open water and a few plants.

Brachydanio rerio (Cyprinidae)

Common name: Zebra danio
Origin: India
Size: 5cm (2in), female larger
Community tank: Yes
Food: Water fleas, dried food, mosquito larvae
Temperature: 18–25 deg C (64–77 deg F)
Breeding: One of the easiest of the egglayers to breed. Temperature 24 deg C (75 deg F)

Most popular of all the danios, this is an active shoaling fish of the upper water layers. This attractive fish has 2 pairs of sensory barbels, and males are characterised by their slimmer appearance.

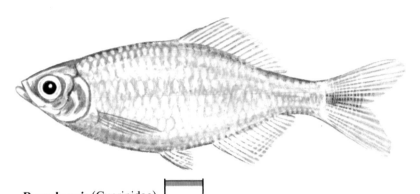

Dano devario (Cyprinidae)

Origin: North West India
Size: 10cm (4in)
Community tank: Yes, kept with medium-sized fish
Food: *Tubifex*, water fleas, flies, dried food
Temperature: 20–24 deg C (68–75 deg F)
Breeding: Fairly easy to breed

A chunky species of the upper water layers. Prefers to live as a shoal in tanks with strong plants and with open water for swimming. Females are less brightly coloured than males. Not commonly seen.

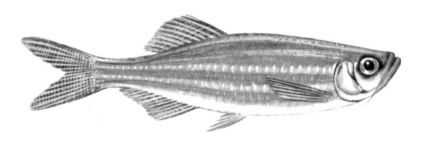

Danio malabaricus (Cyprinidae)

Common name: Giant danio
Origin: India, Malabar, Sri Lanka
Size: 10cm (4in), female larger
Community tank: Yes, as a shoal with fish of similar size
Food: *Tubifex*, water fleas, flies, dried food
Temperature: 20–24 deg C (68–75 deg F)

Breeding: Easy. Temperature 26.5 deg C (80 deg F). Eggs are adhesive

For best effect, this active species should be kept as a shoal, where their colours, as they swim in the upper water layers, are a beautiful sight.

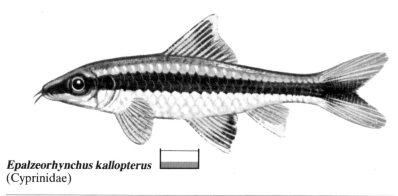

Epalzeorhynchus kallopterus
(Cyprinidae)

Common name: Flying fox
Origin: Borneo, Indonesia, Java, Sumatra
Size: 9cm (3½in)
Community tank: Yes
Food: *Tubifex*, water fleas, algae, dried food
Temperature: 24 deg C (75 deg F)
Breeding: Not known to have bred in captivity

An attractively coloured, elongated fish living near the bottom, where it feeds mainly by scraping algae from rocks and plants. A hardy fish that often chases, or is chased by, other active fish such as sharks. This is done playfully rather than agressively, and injury rarely results.

Labeo bicolor (Cyprinidae)

Common name: Red-tailed black shark
Origin: Thailand
Size: 13cm (5in), female larger
Community tank: Yes
Food: *Tubifex*, dried food, mosquito larvae, algae
Temperature: 22–25.5 deg C (72–78 deg F)

Breeding: Very difficult

Not a true shark at all, this long-lived species is the most popular of the group kept by aquarists. It likes rockwork and roots among which to hide, and can be boisterous in defence of its territory.

Rasbora borapetensis (Cyprinidae)

Origin: Thailand
Size: 6cm (2½in)
Community tank: Yes
Food: *Tubifex*, water fleas, mosquito larvae, dried food
Temperature: 20–25.5 deg C (68–78 deg F)
Breeding: Fairly difficult. Temperature 26.5 deg C (80 deg F). Adhesive eggs

A lively swimmer, although it tends to congregate in peaceful shoals. Beautifully marked, females are stouter than males. This species, although liking scattered vegetation, needs plenty of open water for swimming.

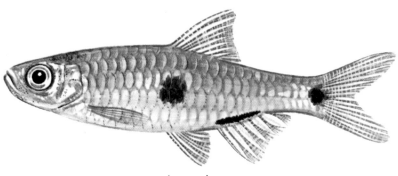

Rasbora elegans (Cyprinidae)

Common name: Elegant rasbora
Origin: Malay Peninsula
Size: 13cm (5in), female larger
Community tank: Yes
Food: *Tubifex*, water fleas, mosquito larvae, dried food
Temperature: 24–25 deg C (75–77 deg F)

Breeding: Fairly difficult. Temperature 28 deg C (82 deg F)

A large, attractive rasbora which swims actively in peaceful shoals. This fish is best kept with other larger inhabitants. Likes plenty of open water for swimming.

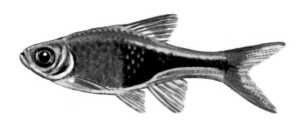

Rasbora heteromorpha (Cyprinidae)

Common name: Harlequin fish
Origin: Sumatra
Size: 4.5cm (1¾in)
Community tank: Yes
Food: Dried food, *Tubifex*, water fleas
Temperature: 22–25 deg C (72–77 deg F)

Breeding: Rather difficult.
Temperature 26.5 deg C (80 deg F)

Probably the most popular rasbora, harlequin fish are lively and peaceful, and are at their best when swimming in a shoal. An ideal fish for a community aquarium.

Rasbora maculata (Cyprinidae)

Common name: Spotted rasbora, Pygmy rasbora
Origin: Malaysia, Indo China, Malacca
Size: 2.5cm (1in)
Community tank: Yes, but only with small or very peaceful fish
Food: *Tubifex*, water fleas, dried food
Temperature: 22.5–25 deg C (73–77 deg F)

Breeding: Moderately easy.
Temperature 26.5 deg C (80 deg F)
Feed fry egg yolk emulsion

The smallest of the rasboras, it may become bullied if large inhabitants of other species share the tank. Males are usually thinner, with a more pronounced reddish hue to the body.

Rasbora pauciperforata
(Cyprinidae)

Common name: Red-striped rasbora, Glowlight rasbora
Origin: Sumatra
Size: 6cm (2½in)
Community tank: Yes
Food: _Tubifex_, water fleas, dried food
Temperature: 21–25 deg C (70–77 deg F)

Breeding: Very difficult

A sleek fish, whose body colours are set off by an iridescent golden-red line along the sides of the body. Peaceful but shy, this fish prefers to swim in shoals in the middle water layers.

Rasbora trilineata (Cyprinidae)

Common name: Scissor-tail
Origin: Malay peninsula
Size: 7.5cm (3in)
Community tank: Yes, with plenty of open water for swimming. Prefers middle water layers
Food: _Tubifex_, water fleas, mosquito larvae, dried food
Temperature: 22–25 deg C (72–77 deg F)

Breeding: Fairly easy. Temperature 26.5 deg C (80 deg F)

This fish derives its name from its habit of twitching its tail in a scissor-like manner as it moves through the water. By nature a shoaling fish of the upper water layers, this fish will take food from the surface.

Tanichthys albonubes (Cyprinidae)

Common name: White-cloud mountain minnow
Origin: China
Size: 5cm (2in), female larger
Community tank: Yes, prefers upper water layers
Food: *Tubifex*, water fleas, dried food
Temperature: 18–22 deg C (64–72 deg F)

Breeding: One of the easiest of egglayers to breed. Plant fine-leaved plants, and coarse gravel at bottom of tank

This pretty little fish can survive in quite low temperatures, and is really only a borderline 'tropical' species. A peaceful fish of the upper and middle water layers.

Aphyosemion australe australe
(Cyprinodontidae)

Common name: Lyretail, Cape Lopez lyretail, Chocolate lyretail
Origin: West Africa, Gabon
Size: Up to 6cm (2½in), female smaller
Community tank: Yes, with its own kind
Food: Water fleas, mosquito larvae, *Tubifex*
Temperature: 20–24 deg C (68–75 deg F)
Breeding: Moderately easy. Temperature 25.5 deg C (78 deg F). Removable nylon mops are

commonly used as a spawning medium for these fish. Eggs can be removed from mops and stored in shallow water in dishes, where they hatch in two to four weeks

A relatively short-lived fish (1 year–18 months), although rewarding due to its colourful appearance. Females do not have the fin extensions of the males, and are a duller brown. This species prefers middle and lower water layers in tanks with soft, acid water.

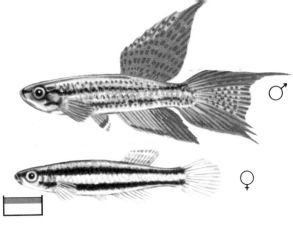

Aphyosemion bivittatum
(Cyprinodontidae)

Common name: Red lyretail
Origin: Tropical West Africa
Size: Up to 6cm (2½in), female smaller
Community tank: Yes, with same species
Food: Water fleas, mosquito larvae, *Tubifex*
Temperature: 20–24 deg C (68–75 deg F)

Breeding: Moderately easy. Temperature 24 deg C (75 deg F). Eggs hatch 12–14 days. The young of this species take 6 months to reach adulthood

An active fish of the upper waters, in which the male is more colourful and has a larger dorsal fin than the female.

Aphyosemion sjoestedti
(Cyprinodontidae)

Common name: Blue gularis
Origin: West Africa (Niger delta)
Size: 11.5cm (4½in)
Community tank: Yes, with similar-sized fish and dim lighting, or species tank
Food: *Tubifex*, water fleas, mosquito larvae, whiteworms
Temperature: 20–24 deg C (68–75 deg F)
Breeding: Needs special care. Bottom spawner. Can be bred by adding handful of boiled peat fibre.

The fish will lay eggs on this; remove once a week and transfer peat with eggs (or just remove eggs) into other containers at 22 deg C (72 deg F). Eggs take 4–6 months to hatch

An extremely attractive but aggressive fish with carnivorous tendencies. The male is characterised by his tri-lobed tail fin; the female is dark olive green with red spots.

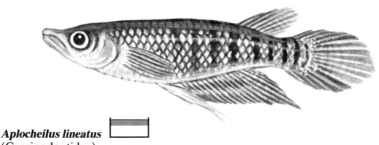

Aplocheilus lineatus
(Cyprinodontidae)

Common name: Striped panchax, Panchax lineatus
Origin: Southern India and Sri Lanka
Size: 10cm (4in), female smaller
Community tank: Yes, with larger fish in well-planted tank
Food: Water fleas, flies, dried food
Temperature: 20–25 deg C (68–77 deg F)
Breeding: Fairly easy. Eggs laid in fine-leaved plants near surface, or can be bred as a mop spawner. One male needs more than one female when spawning. Eggs hatch 10–12 days

This carnivorous, large-mouthed species lives near the surface. Tends to jump out of tank, so tight-fitting lid essential. Male more brightly coloured than female. Largest member of the genus.

Aplocheilus panchax
(Cyprinodontidae)

Common name: Blue panchax
Origin: Burma, India, Malaysia
Size: Up to 8cm (3½in)
Community tank: Yes, with larger fish
Food: Water fleas, flies, dried food
Temperature: 20–25 deg C (68–77 deg F)
Breeding: Easy. Eggs are laid in fine-leaved plants near surface, or can be bred as a mop spawner. Eggs hatch 10–12 days

An undemanding fish with many colour variations. This species likes a tank with open water for swimming, and floating and rooted plants for refuge. Surface swimming.

†*Cynolebias belotti*
(Cyprinodontidae)

Common name: Argentine pearl fish
Origin: Brazil
Size: 7.5cm (3in), female smaller
Community tank: No, best kept with own species
Food: *Tubifex*, water fleas
Temperature: 18–26.5 deg C (64–80 deg F)
Breeding: Extremely difficult. Temperature 22 deg C (72 deg F). After spawning the fish should be removed and the water syphoned off leaving ground cover to dry out. After 3 months the aquarium water should be replaced, and the fry hatch out within 48 hours

A short-lived fish which can be aggressive. Only half-grown specimens should be purchased. Females differ in coloration to males, and are smaller.

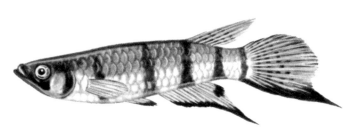

Epiplatys dageti (Cyprinodontidae)

Common name: Red-chinned panchax
Origin: West Africa (Monrovia)
Size: 6cm (2½in), female smaller
Community tank: Yes, but not with small fish
Food: *Tubifex*, dried food, small fishes
Temperature: 21–26.5 deg C (70–80 deg F)
Breeding: Can be bred. Temperature 24.5 deg C (76 deg F). Eggs are deposited on plants over a period of 2–3 weeks. Fry hatch in 1–3 weeks

An active, but peaceful fish, of the upper water layers. The male is a very pretty fish with attractive fins; the female is somewhat duller. Will readily eat small fish.

Jordanella floridae
(Cyprinodontidae)

Common name: American flag fish
Origin: Florida
Size: 5.5cm (2¼in), female larger
Community tank: Yes, with similar-sized fish
Food: _Tubifex_, water fleas, mosquito larvae, dried food
Temperature: 19–22 deg C (66–72 deg F)
Breeding: Moderately easy.

Temperature 24 deg C (75 deg F). Remove female after spawning. Male protects eggs

A bright coloured, stocky specimen with a body pattern extending into the fins. This fish is somewhat aggressive, and favours a heavily planted tank, with open water for swimming.

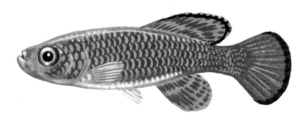

†_Nothobranchius guentheri_
(Cyprinodontidae)

Origin: East Africa
Size: Female 4cm (1½in), male 4.5cm (1¾in)
Community tank: No, species tank only, with sparse vegetation
Food: _Tubifex_, mosquito larvae, water fleas, small fishes, dried food
Temperature: 20–25.5 deg C (68–78 deg F)
Breeding: Moderately easy. Egg

burier. After spawning, remove fish, drain tank for 12 weeks, refill and await hatching. Growth after hatching is rapid

An extremly attractive but short-lived fish with a quarrelsome temperament. Males are larger and more colourful than females.

Pachypanchax playfairii
(Cyprinodontidae)

Origin: Seychelles, East Africa
Size: 10cm (4in), males larger
Community tank: Yes, with medium-sized peaceful fish but with dense vegetation so subordinate fish can hide
Food: _Tubifex_, water fleas, mosquito larvae, small fishes, occasionally it will accept dried food
Temperature: 24 deg C (75 deg F)
Breeding: Moderately easy.

Temperature 25 deg C (77 deg F). Needs a well planted tank, as eggs are attached to floating plants. Adults will eat eggs

An attractive and robust fish, but with a tendency to bully other inhabitants. Prefers upper and middle water layers. The scales of this species tend to stand away from the body slightly. Not very active.

†_Pterolebias peruensis_
(Cyprinodontidae)

Origin: Peru
Size: Male 7.5cm (3in), female 5cm (2in)
Community tank: Species tank preferable
Food: _Tubifex_, water fleas, mosquito larvae
Temperature: 22–25 deg C (72–77 deg F)
Breeding: Moderately easy. This fish

buries its eggs which hatch after 16 weeks, if dried out, or up to 28 weeks if kept wet

An active and rather aggressive fish, this species tends to be fairly short-lived. Males have elongated flag-like tails and are more colourful than females.

♂

♀

Rivulus cylindraceus
(Cyprinodontidae)

Origin: Cuba, Florida
Size: 6cm (2½in)
Community tank: No, species tank only
Food: Live food such as water fleas, *Tubifex* and mosquito larvae
Temperature: 24 deg C (75 deg F)
Breeding: Easy. Temperature 25.5 deg C (78 deg F). One of the egg-hangers which will breed readily on floating plants or mops placed in the tank. Adhesive eggs hatch in 10–14 days

These fish, which sometimes lie on top of floating leaves, need a well-planted tank, otherwise they dash about madly. Close-fitting covers are required on the tanks, since this species has a tendency to jump out of the water. Males have brighter coloration than females.

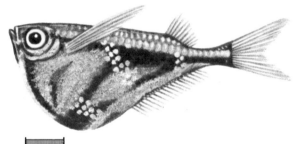

Carnegiella strigata
(Gasteropelecidae)

Common name: Marbled hatchet fish
Origin: Amazon, Guyana
Size: 5cm (2in)
Community tank: Yes
Food: Water fleas, dried food
Temperature: 22.5–26.5 deg C (73–80 deg F)
Breeding: Very difficult. Temperature 26.5 deg C (80 deg F). Well planted tank

A beautiful, unusually shaped species whose common name is derived from the hatchet-like shape of the body. A fish of the surface water layers, it has a tendency to jump clear of the tank, so a well-fitting lid is essential. Not very active and rather shy, it may be harrassed or bullied unless care is taken in selecting the other occupants of the aquarium.

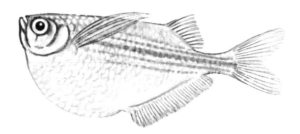

Gasteropelecus levis
(Gasteropelecidae)

Common name: Silver hatchet fish
Origin: Guyana, Amazon Basin
Size: 6cm (2½in)
Community tank: Yes
Food: *Tubifex*, water fleas, flies, dried food
Temperature: 23–28 deg C (73–82 deg F)

Breeding: Not known to have bred in captivity

A delicate, surface-living fish with a tendency, like other hatchet fish, to jump out of the tank. A close-fitting lid is therefore essential. May be bullied or worried by other fish.

Brachygobius xanthozona
(Gobiidae)

Common name: Bumblebee goby
Origin: Sumatra, Java and Borneo
Size: 4cm (1½in), female larger
Community tank: Yes
Food: *Tubifex*, water fleas
Temperature: 24–26.5 deg C (75–80 deg F)
Breeding: Can be bred. Temperature 28 deg C (82 deg F). Eggs laid among plants. Fry eat live food

A territorial fish of the lower and middle water layers, and possessing an unusual body shape. It likes rockwork and plant roots in which to hide. Regular live food necessary for good health.

Nannostomus marginatus
(Hemiodontidae)

Common name: Dwarf pencil fish
Origin: South America, Amazon,
Guyana
Size: 3.5cm (1¼in)
Community tank: Yes
Food: *Tubifex*, water fleas, dried
food
Temperature: 22–26.5 deg C (72–80
deg F)
Breeding: Difficult. Temperature
26.5 deg C (80 deg F). Adults tend to
eat the eggs

A shy, peaceful fish which needs a
well-planted tank where it swims in
all water layers. This fish possesses
interesting body markings. One of
the more colourful of the
Nannostomus species. Not very
active, but even when stationary its
pectoral fins can be seen beating
rapidly to keep it 'hovering' in one
place: when frightened, it moves
very rapidly.

Nannostomus trifasciatus
(Hemiodontidae)

Common name: Three-banded
pencil fish
Origin: Amazon
Size: 4.5cm (1¾in)
Community tank: Yes, with other
peaceful species
Food: *Tubifex*, water fleas, dried
food
Temperature: 22–26.5 deg C (72–80
deg F)

Breeding: Difficult. Temperature 24
deg C (75 deg F). Eggs hatch in 2–3
days

The most attractive of the
Nannostomus species, this is a shy
and quiet fish of the upper and
middle water layers.

†*Monodactylus argenteus*
(Monodactylidae)

Common name: Malayan angel, Mono
Origin: Malaysia, East Africa, North Australia
Size: 13cm (5in)
Community tank: Best amongst scats and its own kind, with roots and rocks for decoration
Food: *Tubifex*, whiteworms, water fleas, shrimps, dried food
Temperature: 24–26.5 deg C (75–80 deg F)

Breeding: Not known to have bred in captivity

This is a fish of brackish water in its natural habitat, and although it can be kept in fresh water, it thrives better in tanks which have had an amount of sea-salt added (1 rounded tablespoon per gallon of water). A peaceful, shoaling fish with a resemblance to angel fish.

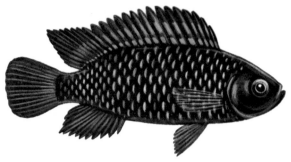

Badis badis (Nandidae)

Common name: Badis
Origin: India
Size: 7.5cm (3in)
Community tank: Yes, with plenty of hiding places
Food: *Tubifex*, water fleas, worms
Temperature: 20–26.5 deg C (68–80 deg F)
Breeding: Can be bred. Temperature 25 deg C (77 deg F). Male becomes aggressive at this time, and guards the eggs and fry. Female should be removed after spawning. Fry must be fed on infusoria (minute organisms)

A charming fish once known as the chameleon fish for its ability to change colour to suit its surroundings. Prefers lower water layers. Females are less colourful.

†***Xenomystus nigri*** (Notopteridae)

Common name: Knife fish
Origin: Central and East Africa
Size: 20.5cm (8in)
Community tank: Not recommended
Food: *Tubifex*, small worms, water fleas, mosquito larvae, snails
Temperature: 24–26.5 deg C (75–80 deg F)
Breeding: Not known to have bred in captivity

A predatory fish with a secretive, noctural way of life. It prefers a dimly lit tank with plenty of plants and rockwork, but open water for swimming. The fish is characterised by the complete absence of a dorsal fin. May be kept with certain large, hardy species including barbs, non-aggressive cichlids and catfish.

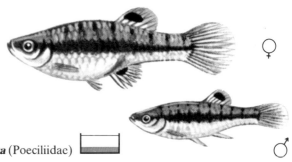

Heterandria formosa (Poeciliidae)

Common name: Mosquito fish
Origin: North Carolina to Florida
Size: Up to 3.5cm (1¼in)
Community tank: Due to their small size they are best kept only with their own kind, or else with peaceful fish such as pencil fish and small tetras
Food: Water fleas, brine shrimps, algae, dried food
Temperature: 20–24 deg C (68–75 deg F)
Breeding: Easy. Temperature 25.5 deg C (78 deg F). Live-bearing; young delivered at the rate of 2 or 3 a day during a period of about 10 days. Parents and young can be left together in a well-planted aquarium

The name mosquito fish is a reference to its very small size, rather than to its diet. This fish is in fact the smallest of the live bearers, and care must be taken not to include any fish in the aquarium that could be a danger to it. Inactive, and spends most of the time in the lower levels of the aquarium.

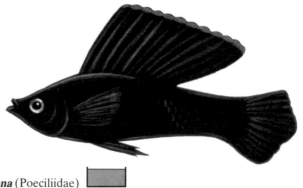

Poecilia latipinna (Poeciliidae)

Common name: Sailfin molly
Origin: Eastern USA
Size: 10cm (4in)
Community tank: Yes
Food: Dried food, water fleas, mosquito larvae, algae, lettuce
Temperature: 22.5–26.5 deg C (73–80 deg F), with a little added sea-salt (1 heaped teaspoonful per gallon of water)

Breeding: Easy in well planted tanks. Bears live young

A beautiful fish with a large dorsal fin, this species is available in several colour varieties. Males can be aggressive towards each other. Prefers a tank with robust plants and open water for swimming.

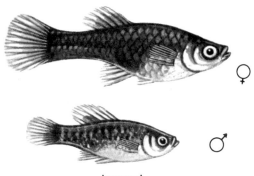

Poecilia melanogaster (Poeciliidae)

Common name: Black-bellied limia
Origin: Jamaica
Size: 6cm (2½in), male smaller
Community tank: Yes
Food: *Tubifex*, mosquito larvae,
dried food
Temperature: 24 deg C (75 deg F)

Breeding: Easy. Temperature 25.5
deg C (78 deg F). Bears live young

A peaceful fish; the male of the
species being smaller than the female
and more brightly hued.

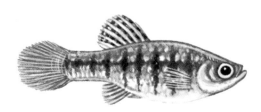

Poecilia nigrofasciata (Poeciliidae)

Common name: Humpbacked limia
Origin: Haiti
Size: 6cm (2½in), male smaller
Community tank: Yes, a peaceful
fish
Food: Mosquito larvae, dried food
Temperature: 24 deg C (75 deg F)

Breeding: Easy. Temperature 25.5
deg C (78 deg F). Bears live young

A peaceful, mid-water swimming
species, attractively marked but not
brightly coloured. Not commonly
seen.

Poecilia reticulata (Poeciliidae)

Common name: Guppy
Origin: Trinidad, Venezuela
Size: Males to 4cm (1½in), female to 6cm (2½in)
Community tank: Yes
Food: *Tubifex*, water fleas, mosquito larvae, dried food
Temperature: 16–25.5 deg C (61–78 deg F)
Breeding: Easy. Temperature 24.5 deg C (76 deg F). Prolific breeder, gives birth to 5–60 live young

The best known of all tropical fish. Available in a wide variety of colours and finnage, this hardy and active species likes open water for swimming. Males bear a characteristic gonopodium, and are much more colourful and smaller than females. Not very long-lived, usually 12–18 months.

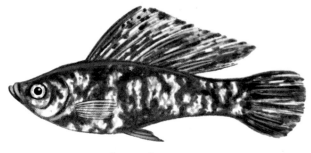

Poecilia sphenops (Poeciliidae)

Common name: Molly
Origin: North America, parts of South America
Size: 6cm (2½in), female larger
Community tank: Yes, a peaceful fish
Food: Water fleas, mosquito larvae, algae, lettuce, dried food
Temperature: 22.5–26.5 deg C (73–80 deg F), with a little added sea salt (1 heaped teaspoonful per gallon of water)

Breeding: Easy. Temperature 26.5 deg C (80 deg F). Hard water preferred, bears live young. Gravid females (those full of young) should not be disturbed, otherwise the young might be born dead

Mollies are peaceful shoaling fish of the upper water layers. Females are stouter than males, which bear a gonopodium.

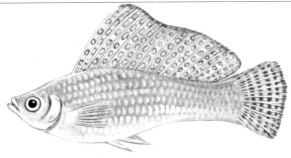

Poecilia velifera (Poeciliidae)

Common name: Sailfin molly
Origin: Yucatan
Size: 13cm (5in)
Community tank: Yes, but the males can be aggressive towards each other
Food: Dried food, water fleas, mosquito larvae, algae, lettuce
Temperature: 22.5–26.5 deg C (73–80 deg F), with a little added sea-salt (1 heaped teaspoonful per gallon of water)

Breeding: Easy. Temperature 26.5 deg C (80 deg F). Hard water preferred

An active and hardy species which prefers a well-planted tank with rockwork, and open water for swimming. Males can be aggressive towards each other, and feature a very tall dorsal fin.

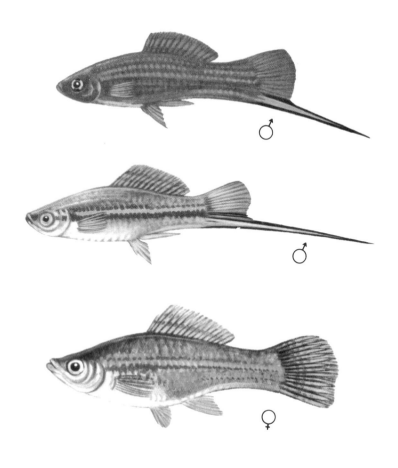

Xiphophorus helleri (Poeciliidae)

Common name: Swordtail
Origin: East Mexico
Size: 7.5cm (3in)
Community tank: Yes
Food: *Tubifex*, water fleas, mosquito larvae, dried food
Temperature: 17–25 deg C (63–77 deg F)
Breeding: Easy. Temperature 25.5–26.5 deg C (78–80 deg F). Interesting courtship behaviour. 75–100 live young per brood.

Females have the amazing ability of turning into males

The sword-like extension of the male's tail fin makes these very colourful and extremely popular fish immediately recognisable. A lively species, but the males become rather aggressive to each other and sometimes to other small inhabitants of the aquarium.

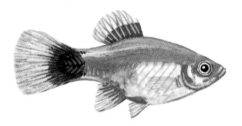

Xiphophorus maculatus (Poeciliidae)

Common name: Platy
Origin: East Mexico, Guatemala
Size: 4cm (1½in)
Community tank: Yes
Food: _Tubifex_, water fleas, mosquito larvae, dried food
Temperature: 20–25 deg C (68–77 deg F)
Breeding: Easy. Temperature 25.5 deg C (78 deg F). Bears live young

This fish has a stocky body, and lacks the sword-like tail extension of _X. helleri_. An active but peaceful species preferring a densely planted tank, but with some open water for swimming. One of the best livebearers for a community aquarium, available in a wide range of colour varieties.

Xiphophorus variatus (Poeciliidae)

Common name: Variatus platy
Origin: East Mexico
Size: 7.5cm (3in), male smaller
Community tank: Yes, with some dense vegetation
Food: _Tubifex_, water fleas, mosquito larvae, dried food
Temperature: 17–25 deg C (63–77 deg F)
Breeding: Easy. Temperature 25.5 deg C (78 deg F). Prolific breeder bearing live young. Both sexes have

a dark patch at the rear of the abdomen, which should not be confused with the gravid spot (of variable density) seen on most female livebearers

A variable species which interbreeds readily with _X. maculatus_. Lively and hardy, it likes dense vegetation, but some open water for swimming. The male is rather more brightly coloured than the female.

†*Scatophagus argus* (Scatophagidae)

Common name: Scat
Origin: East Indies
Size: 10cm (4in)
Community tank: No, should be kept on its own, or with other brackish-water fish
Food: *Tubifex*, water fleas, mosquito larvae, dried food
Temperature: 22–26.5 deg C (72–80 deg F); water with added sea-salt

Breeding: Not known to have bred in captivity

A timid fish which can be taught in time to take food from your fingers. Has a tendency to eat aquarium plants. Although peaceful it can be an aggressive feeder.

Kryptopterus bicirrhis (Siluridae)

Common name: Glass catfish
Origin: Indonesia, South-east Asia
Size: Up to 10cm (4in)
Community tank: Yes, but not with very small fish
Food: *Tubifex*, water fleas, whiteworms, mosquito larvae
Temperature: 20–25.5 deg C (68–78 deg F)
Breeding: Not known to have bred in captivity

A most unusual fish of lower and middle water layers, in which the transparent body can be seen to house the internal organs in a silvery sac. Swims in a characteristic 'tail-down' manner. One pair of long sensory barbels. Although secretive and not particularly lively its presence can act as a useful foil to the more traditional active species.

†*Toxotes jaculator* (Toxotidae)

Common name: Archer fish
Origin: Southern Asia, China, India, Australia, Phillipines
Size: 10cm (4in)
Community tank: No, species tank with plants growing up above surface
Food: Flies, small crickets, may accept *Tubifex* and water fleas. Difficult to feed in captivity
Temperature: 25–26.5 deg C (77–80 deg F) with added sea salt (1 heaped teaspoonful per gallon of water)

Breeding: Not known to have bred in captivity

An extremely unusual perch-like fish which is sometimes difficult to feed in captivity. In the wild, it obtains its food by squirting a jet of water at insects on overhanging plant matter. The insects fall into the water and are eaten. Fairly shy and peaceful.

Index